The Rise of the
HUMANS

The Rise of the
HUMANS

How to outsmart the digital deluge

Dave Coplin

HARRIMAN HOUSE LTD

3A Penns Road
Petersfield
Hampshire
GU32 2EW
GREAT BRITAIN
Tel: +44 (0)1730 233870

Email: enquiries@harriman-house.com

Website: www.harriman-house.com

First published in Great Britain in 2014 by Harriman House.

ISBN: 9780857194053

British Library Cataloguing in Publication Data

A CIP catalogue record for this book can be obtained from the British Library.

Illustrations by DocktorBob (www.docktorbob.com)

Set in Segoe and Dante MT

'The most exciting breakthroughs of the 21st century will not occur because of technology but because of an expanding concept of what it means to be human.'

– JOHN NAISBITT

For John: Remember, computers can only give you answers.
Take time to find the right questions.

As a buyer of the printed book of *The Rise of the Humans*, you can download the full eBook free of charge. Simply point your smartphone or tablet camera at this QR code or go to:

ebooks.harriman-house.com/TROTH

Contents

About the Author

DAVE COPLIN is the Chief Envisioning Officer for Microsoft UK and an established thought leader in the UK. He has worked across a wide range of industries and customers, providing strategic advice and guidance around the intersection of a modern society and technology both inside and outside of the world of work. Dave is passionate about turning the base metal of technology into valuable

Author photo © CTK Photobank/Rene Fluger

assets that affect the way we live, work and play and, in so doing, move the focus from the technology itself to the outcome it enables.

His previous book, *Business Reimagined*, provided individuals and organisations with a view of a new working environment based on collaborative and flexible working and on technology that, used correctly, liberates rather than constrains.

Dave has contributed to a range of media articles, conferences and forums all relating to the goal of making technology less "visible" and more "valuable" in our daily lives.

www.theenvisioners.com | @dcoplin

Introduction

DO YOU EVER feel like we're missing the point of technology?

A few years ago, I was with some colleagues and we were lamenting how technology no longer seemed to be anything special. As a group of people employed in the technology industry, this was obviously pretty alarming.

Since technology was no longer new to the world of work or our personal lives, telling people more stories about the technology itself suddenly seemed – at least for a conference-bar-fuelled afternoon – to be wrong. Not to mention a bit dull.

But that was actually a problem with us, not with technology. And it's a pretty common problem. I think we've all felt it at times. It was a problem with how we've always done things: technology is now advancing many times more quickly than the world in which we live, and old ways of doing things sometimes leave little room for technology to have the kind of impact it's really able to. We get bored of it, but only because we've hardly opened ourselves up to half of what it can do.

This was at the heart of my previous book, *Business Reimagined*. One of the places most superficially transformed – but least *actually* altered – by technology is the world of work. And it is beginning to cause serious problems: again and again, studies show a majority of workers disaffected and unproductive in the office. My theory was that this was only getting worse, despite living in an apparently enlightened age of open-plan productivity, because employees used to the connectivity and speed of technology in their private lives were butting up against broken, old-fashioned ways of doing things that just had no room for the fullness of technology.

Also, open-plan offices are rubbish.

So, above all I set out to try and nudge organisations and individuals to embrace the potential of technology and to recognise the constraints that past experience placed on what we think we can do – and move past them. The book called for firms and individuals to reimagine their own businesses and the way they work.

The materials with which to refashion those businesses – the technology that seemed so boring, or irrelevant, or limited – was already very much to hand, and being used by creative individuals and organisations in ways that were anything *but* boring.

The story didn't really end there, though. The more I got into that conversation, the more I realised that, whichever way you look at it, it is what my dad calls the 'interface between the keyboard and the chair' – the human being – that ultimately holds the keys to our success or failure.

We cannot solve the problems we face through technology alone. Given we are now supplied with more technology and data than ever before – a veritable digital deluge – our future lies in our ability to harness not hate it.

Hate is maybe a bit strong, but I don't know anybody who doesn't increasingly despair at the volume of information coming at them, or at the seemingly inescapable nature of our digital world. Don't get me wrong: this is not about bad technology. It's about bad usage.

The incredible transformative devices and services that now populate our world have changed many things for the better, but our ability to really see and reach out for the full potential these things offer (or even sometimes just use them appropriately) is often overwhelmed by the pace of our lives and the rate of change.

This book is my attempt to start answering this problem: it's a call to action, not to despair as we fall beneath the waves of endless data and connectivity, but for individuals and organisations to adapt to survive it – and then to take advantage of the opportunities that it places at their feet every single day. The digital deluge can start by sounding like a scary thing. But it ends by being incredibly exciting.

As we begin to understand it more, this opportunity will change what it means to be a customer, to be an employee or an employer. As we'll see, it will even change what it means to be human.

When it comes to this potential we can no longer afford the luxury of ignorance or fear. We must understand that the digital deluge is not a threat but a gift to society – but it will be up to us to rise to the challenge to make it work.

Dave Coplin
London, 2014

OF COURSE, I BLAME Alexander Graham Bell.[1] After all, he started it. It was his work back in the late 19th century that enabled the connection of two geographically separated individuals by transforming their interactions into electronic signals and stuffing them down a length of metal wire.

---

1   You can blame Elisha Gray if you like.

Bell's invention of the telephone marked the beginning of an incredible change in our society. And it's a change that is far from over. Today it is taking shape in new and unexpected ways.

Over the last ten years the nature of this technology has altered dramatically. I don't just mean that modern smartphones don't work by using a combination of telegraph wire and metal reeds (if yours does, it's probably time for an upgrade). What's changed is that we no longer just use technology to connect ourselves with other people separated by large distances. Instead, we are increasingly using it to connect when the distances are inconsequential.

We sit at our open-plan desks, emailing the person next to us just to figure out where we're going to grab lunch. We use instant messaging to replace water-cooler gossip, and we even use our mobile phones to call or text down from the bedroom to order tea and toast when it's our turn for the lie-in.

In other words, technology designed to help humans communicate is making them communicate in ways that are less than human.

As we will see, this is part of a significant trend affecting happiness, productivity – even health. Technology's ease and omnipresence is not just making things more impersonal. All those satellite-enabled breakfast requests are part of something much larger – a swiftly rising tide of data, pouring in from a seemingly endless ocean of interaction and information. It's submerging not just whole industries but lives, with millions of us getting lost at sea both at home and at work.

It's at this point in a book like this that the author would usually introduce a nice pretty graph, typically a line chart showing the explosive growth of information over the past few decades. Sure, I could have picked one of a hundred different examples, but to be honest, dear reader, all of the graphs are the same, it really doesn't matter which one you choose. They're all "up and to the right", and as they get further out, the curve just gets steeper and steeper.

The strength of the virtual world, it seems, is disconnecting us from the real world.

THE LIE OF MULTI-TASKING

So you've read the opening. Nice one! But how far did you get before you had the urge to check your phone or flip to another app to see what was happening on your social network?

Maybe you felt a phantom buzz in your pocket from the phone that you now realise is on the table beside you, or perhaps you got distracted by one of a hundred different notifications you have set to tell you when there's new email, breaking news, changes in the weather, public transport, or even when it's time to hydrate.

You tell yourself, 'It's OK, it's no big deal. I can flip between all of these things because I am a modern human. I can multi-task!' And therein lies the first big issue we face – the lie of multi-tasking.

When I was a kid I used to have endless arguments with my parents about my 'incredible cognitive ability', because not only was I able to listen to music and do my homework simultaneously, but the addition of the secondary task actually helped my concentration on the primary one.

After all, I'd spent hours labouring over a hot tape-deck listening to the Sunday evening chart show, painstakingly hovering over the pause and record buttons to make sure I could anticipate the end of the song. I felt I'd earned the right to rock out to Duran Duran's "Hungry Like the Wolf" while grappling with some of the more arduous elements of simultaneous equations, or the complexities of crop rotation in the 14th century.

And we now know that I sort of had a point (sorry, Mum).

Many studies have shown that listening to the right music can help individuals reach "flow state" and help creativity and concentration.[2] The brain, it seems, can be encouraged by the right stimuli to operate in different or enhanced ways. Listening to music causes the brain to generate alpha and theta waves that induce creativity.

But, importantly, it's about finding the *right* stimuli, and a balance is crucial. Attempt much more than background music and things quickly fall apart.

And these days, the balance is no longer about primary and secondary tasks. Today's heavy multi-tasker juggles listening to music with browsing the web, running an app, having a conversation over IM, and watching TV alongside the actual task at hand – be it homework or business. Although they tell you they're pretty good at it, the reality is we're simply not, and this time the proof is scientific (sorry, son).

Multi-tasking is such an accepted part of our everyday lives (both at work and at home) that we've forgotten it's actually

---

2   Dabul, Vanesa (12 March 2014), "How Music Affects the Human Brain", *LIVESTRONG.COM*. **www.livestrong.com/article/157461-how-music-affects-the-human-brain**

a very recent concept. Originally coined in the mid-60s by a bunch of computer scientists, multi-tasking is an idea based on the world of computing. It referred to a method of computing where multiple tasks are performed at the same time rather than one after another. So it's an entirely digital, not human, concept.

Our ability as humans to do multiple tasks simultaneously is restricted by the basic reality of how our brains work, not our individual mental capabilities or our gender.

Plenty of research proves this; one of my favourite studies is from Professor Clifford Nass and his team at Stanford University.[3] They monitored a large group of students to see how they coped with constant switching from task to task – whether it was filtering irrelevant information or using their working memory.

The result?

People who spent a lot of time multi-tasking were particularly abysmal at dealing with the workload.[4] Even worse, another study by Professor Nass showed that teenage girls who multi-tasked on multiple devices were stunted in their social and emotional development compared to girls who focused on talking to friends face-to-face.

Doing more, it seems, often means doing less.

---

3   Sullivan, Kathleen J. (4 November 2013), "Professor Clifford I. Nass, expert on human/computer interactions, dead at 55", *Stanford Report* (Stanford, California). **news.stanford.edu/news/2013/november/cliff-nass-obit-110413**

4   Gorlick, Adam (24 August 2009), "Media multitaskers pay mental price, Stanford study shows", *Stanford Report* (Stanford, California). **news.stanford.edu/news/2009/august24/multitask-research-study-082409**

Nass, Clifford and Raeburn, Paul (28 August 2009), "Multitasking May Not Mean Higher Productivity", *Talk of the Nation* (NPR). **www.npr.org/templates/story/story.php?storyId=112334449**

Multi-taskers are, 'suckers for irrelevancy, everything distracts them', says Nass, who warns that companies that force their employees to multi-task are actually creating an occupational health hazard – 'It's not safe for people's brains'.

This is just one of the studies that shows how 'multi-tasking is going to be problematic for people, that it does compromise productivity', says Dr David W. Goodman, the director of the Adult Attention Deficit Disorder Center of Maryland in Baltimore.[5]

We've all seen or experienced this in action at work. I'm not saying that employers necessarily force employees to work in this way, but the fast-moving pace of business and the overflowing (and often misused) means of communication in our working world leads to an inevitable temptation for the individual to try and make more from less.

How many times have you sat in a meeting claiming that you are taking "notes" on your laptop when you've actually been "catching up on email while the deathly boring meeting continues around me", or at least have been sat in a meeting room with others who were doing this? It's not hard to see how ineffective this is, not just in terms of the contribution of an individual in a meeting, but much more importantly in the point of having a meeting at all.

There's a simple explanation for humans failing to do multiple things at once: the brain has a physical limit. When we multi-task, each task is assigned to one half of our brain, and for tasks that have low cognitive load, it feels like we can cope.

---

5   Tamkins, Theresa (25 August 2009), "Drop that BlackBerry! Multitasking may be harmful", *CNN.com/health*. **edition.cnn.com/2009/HEALTH/08/25/multitasking.harmful**

But when the tasks require more attention or there are more of them, that higher load soon places demands on our brains that we simply can't deliver on. Essentially, we run out of grey matter to do the job.

When it comes to multi-tasking, one plus one does not quite equal two.

'Anyone who brags of being a multi-tasker', says Paul Pearsall, author of *Toxic Success*, 'is confessing to being a sufferer of toxic success syndrome. Research indicates that multi-tasking is another name for attention deficit disorder, and people that succumb lack productivity and effectiveness.'[6]

THE DIGITAL DISTRACTION

Not being able to multi-task wouldn't be such a problem if it wasn't for the way in which technology has changed the demands on our attention.

The more connected we are, the more people we connect with, the more information we create and subsequently have to consume. But this doesn't just raise the volume of data (by one estimate the average person receives 63,000 words of information a day – twice the length of this book). Disruption levels are also rising, whether thanks to company-wide email, text messages or social network posts from our friends and colleagues. And even without all that, we're getting really good at using those same things to distract ourselves.

---

6   Pearsall, Paul (2002), *Toxic Success: How to Stop Striving and Start Thriving* (Inner Ocean Publishing, Maui).

The typical office worker gets about 11 continuous minutes of work done before an interruption, suggests research by Professor Gloria Mark, who studies digital distraction at the University of California.

When students go online in the classroom, it's as if they've got 'five different magazines, several television shows, some shopping opportunities, and a phone on their desk', says Professor David Cole of Georgetown University.

And what happens once we've been side-tracked? We take a long time to get our act together again.

A few years ago a team of researchers studied some of my Microsoft colleagues in the United States to see what happens when they are interrupted in their tasks by an incoming email or instant message. Once the disruption was dealt with, instead of bouncing straight back into the task they were completing before the interruption, they slowly worked their way back through a veritable smorgasbord of information – checking other email or instant messages, and browsing news, sports or entertainment websites.

On average it took them around 15 minutes to return to a serious mental task like writing great computer code or finishing some analysis.

Professor Gloria Mark did similar research and observed even longer delays. In her study it could take up to 23 minutes for a worker to return to his or her original task. Eric Horvitz, distinguished scientist and managing director of Microsoft Research, and one of the co-authors of the Microsoft study, says he was 'surprised how easily people were distracted and how long it took them to get back to the task'.

But in many ways I actually think it's *not* surprising.

Slogging through screens of code, sorting your thoughts for that in-depth analysis, often feel like endless, thankless tasks. It's so much easier to opt for the quick dopamine buzz, the chemical reward produced naturally by our very own brain for instant gratification.

And while just five years ago most of us could still recharge on little islands of calm – during the commute, at the dinner table, or even in front of the television – the rise of smartphones and tablets is now connecting us all day long. For many people their devices are with them from the moment they wake to the moment they fall asleep.

Mobile devices that have undoubtedly 'helped us become more productive...can also serve as round-the-clock distraction', argues John Reed, of Robert Half Technology, who conducted a CIO survey into digital distraction.[7] We have become addicts of the quick high we get when we file email, click "like", or re-tweet a post. And so we have trained our brains to shrink from laborious, "high-fibre" tasks that increase our cognitive capability and further our understanding and insight.

Our daily email, news and social networking buzz is turning out to be more than a time sink. In fact, it's killing our productivity and potential. And the impact is dramatic: instead of opening up new connections, multi-tasking and the digital deluge are threatening to disconnect us. Our use of technology to communicate in our offices and homes is

---

7   Robert Half Technology (7 May 2013), "CIO Survey: Tech Gadgets Contributing to Decline in Workplace Etiquette", *PR Newswire*. **www.prnewswire.com/news-releases/ digital-distraction-cio-survey-tech-gadgets-contributing-to-decline-in-workplace-etiquette-206399621.html**

progressively distancing us from our colleagues, from our friends and families, and worse still, from our very own selves, our thoughts, and even our ability to think.

Recent research commissioned by Microsoft UK, which polled more than 2,000 office workers in the UK, found that 77% consider 'a productive day in the office' as clearing email.

I find this terrifying. Since when did doing email equal work? Sure, email is one of the tools of work, but somehow we've ended up in a place where the tool is viewed as the result or outcome. Partly this stems from our broken modern-day definition of "productivity". As discussed in my first book, *Business Reimagined*, we often now focus on the process of work rather than what it's meant to produce.

But it's also very much because of how we are using technology – and how technology has begun to use us.

My employer did not hire me for my ability to process email or to operate any other particular process. It employed me because it wanted access to the thing between my ears – my brain – not to sign me as a significant addition to a multinational digital ping-pong team.

But over the years, technology has become such a powerful influence that this has got harder and harder for many of us to hold onto. By exploiting some of our weaknesses as humans, technology has helped those weaknesses increasingly control how we communicate, collaborate and work.

And the damage ultimately goes deeper still.

"Dying for Information?", a Reuters survey of 1,300 managers around the world, found that two thirds believe that information overload not only causes a loss of job satisfaction, but also damages personal relationships. One third said it had damaged their health.

According to a 2010 survey by Basex, 94% of those questioned had at some point felt overwhelmed by information to the point of incapacity.[8] The study showed, amongst other things, that 30% of knowledge workers had no time at all for thought and reflection during their day, and 58% had only between 15 and 30 minutes.

This is very alarming stuff.

BEING MINDFUL: TAKING BACK CONTROL

So what's the remedy?

Should we use apps like "Freedom" and "SelfControl" to limit our access to the internet and boost our productivity? Maybe the solution is to deny ourselves digital tools and ban laptops and tablets from the workplace, as professors have done at George Washington University, the University of Virginia and others? Or we could all go the way of Atos, a French IT systems integrator, and ban internal email?

Alexander Graham Bell may have helped start this problem, but he also had his own solution: he refused to have a telephone installed in his study for fear that it would be an intrusion on his work.

---

8   "Managing Information Overload" workshop (22 January 2014), James C. Jernigan Library, Texas A&M University-Kingsville (Kingsville, Texas). **libguides.tamuk.edu/info_overload**

But perhaps the biggest solution already being used is "mindfulness" – the ability to focus our attention and awareness on the things that matter and will make a difference whether at work or play. The idea is to train ourselves to step out of the raging river of information overload and become an impartial spectator who refuses to be overwhelmed by the torrent of data.

Whether it's called "neural self-hacking" or "managing your energy", mindfulness is seen by more and more companies as a strategy that can help their staff cope with the dual stress of multi-tasking and data saturation. Several studies – albeit using only small samples – suggest that courses that teach mindfulness do indeed reduce stress levels and improve social interaction.[9]

And that's great – indeed the principles of mindfulness will underpin a lot of the positive responses and developments we'll be looking at in this book – but on its own it's more of a useful first step. It's not attacking the underlying problem. The digital deluge and the multi-tasking mania carry on much as before, with mindfulness helping us at least not be so overcome by them – but not doing much more.

Is that the best we can hope for?

It's probably better than the other things listed before it, but it can't be the beginning and end of a solution.

Some or all of those other alternatives can be really tempting. A study followed information workers for three days while

9   Hunter, Jeremy (April 2013), "Is mindfulness good for business?", *Mindful* magazine (Foundation for a Mindful Society). **jeremyhunter.net/wp-content/uploads/2013/02/ Mindful-Is-Mindfulness-Good-for-Business.pdf**

they were using email, and for five days when they had to go without. The outcome was startling. After just a few days without email, the workers focused longer on their tasks, multi-tasked less and had lower stress levels.[10] But again, my fear is that abandoning connections is really just giving up on solving the problem – it's turning our backs on the digital problems and therefore missing out on the digital future.

Even simple coping strategies are not long-term solutions. Dr Goodman has some good ideas, including scheduling when you check your email to avoid becoming a slave to the email buzz. And in fact we've always been able to easily control when, where, and how often we are notified of new email coming into our inboxes. My phone beeps, my computer chimes, I can receive little messages or "toasts" pop up to tell me that someone, somewhere, has contacted me. I can switch them all off if I want.

The problem is, we may have these simple switches, but the switches alone aren't enough. We've gone too far, it's changed us too much, and we're always too connected – even if we want to pretend we're not.

When it comes to email notifications, for instance, I'm pretty sure you're like me: I really don't need to know if I've got new email anymore because I can basically guarantee I will always have new email. These days it's the digital equivalent of being reminded that there is air to breathe.

And it's always tempting to pop out for some fresh air, whether I need it or not.

---

10   Mark, Gloria J., Voida, Stephen and Cardello, Armand V. (2012), "A Pace Not Dictated by Electrons: An Empirical Study of Work Without Email", Department of Informatics, University of California, Irvine. **www.ics.uci.edu/~gmark/Home_page/Research_files/CHI%202012.pdf**

In other words, the pervasiveness of mobile devices and connectivity means that the problem is with us wherever we are and whatever we're doing, and the temptation is always going to be there. I can turn off email notifications, but I cannot turn off that part of my mind that knows I'll have new emails.

And, besides, we really don't *want* to kill connectivity – nor eliminate disruption. Connectivity also empowers us. It helps us share, grow, be inspired, and see things with unrivalled context. And disruption isn't always the end of the world. Sometimes disruption is the next big idea – or where the next big idea begins. It could be a conversation that triggers creativity, an interruption that prompts innovation. Sometimes, as we'll see, disruption is serendipity.

So the real question is: *how can we make sure we avoid unhelpful distractions and prevent ourselves from being overwhelmed by connections but don't miss out on the inspiring and useful ones?*

The solutions are going to have to be comprehensive. They have to do more than pretend the problem isn't there or help disguise it for a few hours. And they need to tackle more than just technology. Technology alone, as we've seen, isn't the problem. Instead, used properly and by focusing on the potential of the future rather than the constraints of the past, it should be a large part of the solution.

In order to do this we need to continuously remind ourselves of the transformative potential of the powerful, beautiful, connected devices and services we now have access to. Technology should be a magical, powerful force that can enrich our lives for the better both at work and at play. But it's up to us to make the right decisions to make that possible.

And, actually, even the idea of tackling the problem is ultimately only half the picture. Because a world that is rich in incredible devices, services, data and connections is also one that is full of incredible potential – we should want to do more than just tame its wild waters. Once we've secured ourselves against drowning, we should set our sights on the better shores these seas can take us to.

So, solving the problem of the digital deluge – and going beyond it – is ultimately what this book is about. The exciting news is there *are* solutions out there. There is some remarkable progress being made, and signs already of what a more balanced and productive data-filled future holds, both for individuals and firms. There's work to be done, and pitfalls to avoid – and time may feel like it's up against us – but the future does not need to be feared or forsaken.

The rise of the humans starts here.

Mastering the screaming digital demons, by Gloria Mark

MASTERING THE DIGITAL demons screaming for our attention is the reality of working in our current digital age: people constantly switch information streams and interactions. During our research we tracked people's activities to the second, and found that about every three minutes they switch their attention between different computer applications (word processing, email, internet surfing), people (face-to-face and remote interactions), and devices (cell phone, computer). Switching may be not so bad if you stick to one topic. When I write an academic paper, I can switch between writing and talking to a colleague and going online – if it all concerns the same paper. However, we also

---

discovered that people tend to switch to completely different topics – what we call switching working spheres – which means they stick with one issue for on average about 10.5 minutes. That's not very long, certainly not long enough to engage very deeply with a topic. They barely settle their thoughts on one topic before they're on to the next. This type of cognitive shift is stressful, because we constantly have to make a mental effort to reorient to a new context. Our digital lives become a Brownian motion.

What causes such rapid switching? First, let's consider that there are two ways that people can be interrupted: we interrupt ourselves, or are interrupted by others. The sources of external interruptions are obvious: email notifications, telephones ringing; but why do people self-interrupt? This puzzle falls into place once we consider all the things at work that compete for our attention. We can access any document on our computer, any news report, Facebook, email, any social media site, or for that matter, any of the nearly two billion web pages currently indexed as of 2014. Digital information at our fingertips is very seductive. So as we ponder a better wording for a text we write, why not take a break and see what's new on Facebook? Or what stories have just appeared on *Wired*?

As a scientist, I'm interested in why people self-interrupt. From an observer's perspective, we can identify self-interruptions when a person suddenly stops what they are doing, for example in mid-sentence in a Word document, and turns to do something completely different, such as checking email. Our research shows that periods of high external interruptions are followed by periods of high self-interruptions. This suggests that people may be conditioned to self-interrupt. In other words, the external interruptions we receive through digital media may have created an environment where we have become habituated to interrupt ourselves. We have created a downward spiral where interruptions beget more interruptions.

Interruptions are not always bad. We found during our research that people who expect interruptions can actually end up working faster. In our laboratory, we gave people a simple task – answering a series of emails – to simulate what they might do in their office. When they were interrupted, it actually took them less time to answer the emails (subtracting the time it took to handle the interruption) than when they worked without interruptions. This suggests that people who expect interruptions work faster to compensate for the fact that they know that dealing with interruptions takes time. Interruptions can also be beneficial as they provide a break; for example, setting a problem aside can refresh one's thinking. Sometimes an interruption with a colleague helps people see their work or a particular problem in a different light.

Anecdotally, we know that email is one of the main culprits for interruptions. We decided to test this empirically and cut off an organisation's email for a work week. The result: people were significantly less stressed, could focus longer, and switched tasks less frequently.

We are all caught up in an interconnected web of digital media, people and information. It's like a candy store with unlimited offerings. And we succumb to the digital demons vying for our attention. Mastering information will be the next grand challenge as we trek through our digital age.

Gloria Mark is a professor in the Department of Informatics at the University of California, Irvine.

IF YOU'RE LIKE me, you might be lucky enough to remember a world before personal computers and the internet.

I say "lucky", not because I think wistfully of a simpler time when we were able to pause for thought and the only "information overload" I had to worry about was when we got back from holiday and the paper shop delivered a backlog of *2000 AD* comics that I had to wade through in order to find out what Judge Dredd had been up to in Mega-City One.

It's just that I think it's helpful if you're able to make a reasonable comparison of how things were then with how they are now – it provides a useful starting point for wondering how things could be. It helps you remember that nothing is inevitable; not problems – or progress.

I remember back to my time of study and the hours spent endlessly in the library – the old analogue equivalent of the internet – an environment where (if it was a good library) not only was I surrounded by the best knowledge, insight, opinion and stories our society had amassed, but I was also provided with a librarian, my own personal steward, there to guide me on my journey, helping me to discover the relevant and avoid the irrelevant.

The way we consumed information was also different back then. It was as simple as reading, taking notes and ordering your thoughts in silence; with hours of concentrated study and little distraction.

Today, our access to information is seemingly limitless. Most is digital and searchable, with hardly a book left un-scanned, and a whole new world of opinion, content and facts never more than a click away.

On our digital journey, the librarian is still there, but under a very different guise. Instead of a human being, search engines and their algorithms are in charge of the content I look for, selecting the most appropriate material based not only on the key words I provide, but what I have sought out before.

However, seemingly infinite content, immediate access and search-engine assistance does not exist in a vacuum. Added to modern-day time pressures and work culture, it has given rise to what are the first attempts at responding to the digital deluge.

Unfortunately, these attempts aren't very successful. We have ended up replacing the time we would have spent consuming and (importantly) *digesting* information with time essentially spent acquiring yet more of it. Instead of going deep and giving it some thought, we have succumbed to a culture that alternates between two unhealthy behaviours: information snacking and data bingeing. We're either nibbling in passing or gorging to distraction.

As Nicholas Carr puts it in his controversial book, *The Shallows*: 'we are evolving from being cultivators of personal knowledge to being hunter gatherers in the electronic data forest'. And that is a vulnerable and ultimately unproductive place to be. I am comforted by the fact that this is not an entirely new problem – in his 1967 classic, *The Effective Executive*, Peter Drucker described the need for 'reserving chunks of time for reflection' – but it is a problem that is getting worse.

It would be a mistake to think that laziness is driving this change. Of course, it's much easier to reach for the next tweet or email rather than to think in-depth about what you need to do based on the last one. But in reality, snacking and bingeing on information are actually the two main strategies we naturally use to cope with the torrent of data that's raging at us from the omnipresent glowing rectangles in our lives. They are part surrender and part coping mechanism.

This means they have a lot to teach us about how to truly work our way out of our current predicament. So let's take each in turn.

INFOGESTION

Bingeing is big business. People spend upwards of 11 hours out of every 24 in a state of constant consumption. Not eating, but gorging on information ceaselessly flowing from the screens and speakers we all hold dear.

As Clay A. Johnson says in his book, *The Information Diet*, just as society has grown morbidly obese on sugar, fat and flour, so too have we become gluttons for texts, instant messages, emails, RSS feeds, downloads, videos, status updates and tweets.

Our bingeing on data can take many forms. We endlessly file emails in a pointless attempt to reach the holy grail of inbox zero, and we spend hours exploring all the enticing rabbit holes we come across online rather than focusing on the task at hand.

"Wiki-wasting" is my favourite example of this. Wikipedia is one of the digital wonders of the world, and the ease with which I can jump from one thought or topic to another is such an irresistible distraction that by the time I've finished a Wikipedia session (usually lasting several hours) I can rarely remember the question I was trying to answer in the first place.

Likewise, thanks to on-demand television, we don't just watch one episode of a TV series any more, waiting another seven days to see what happens on "next week's thrilling instalment, same Bat-time, same Bat-channel". Instead, we gorge.

According to research by market leader Netflix, on average we watch 2.3 episodes of any given TV series in the same sitting.[11] In fact, half of all Netflix subscribers actually watch a full season of up to 22 episodes within just one week.[12]

Market researchers at Nielsen report that 'bingeing is the new streaming' across all major video-on-demand services, whether it's Hulu, Netflix or Amazon Prime.[13]

We also try to drink the firehose of Twitter and Facebook feeds, overloading ourselves with information and mistaking quantity for quality (and comprehensiveness for insight) rather than adapting to their new ways of consumption.

Often the bingeing is compounded because we try to use old methods of consumption to ingest new media. For instance, people often initially approach Twitter and Facebook like they approach email. I have this conversation a lot. People who are not yet well into their own journey with social media will look over my shoulder at the torrent of tweets passing across my screen and exclaim 'How on earth do you get the time to read all of those messages?'

---

11   Abbruzzese, Jason (13 December 2013), "Embrace the Binge: Netflix Viewers Average 2.3 Episodes per Sitting", *Mashable* (New York). **mashable.com/2013/12/13/embrace-the-binge-netflix-data-shows-viewers-usually-watch-more-than-one-embargo-til-6am**

12   Jurgensen, John (12 December 2013), "Netflix Says Binge Viewing is No 'House of Cards'", *Wall Street Journal* (New York). **online.wsj.com/news/articles/SB1000142405270230393250457925403101758 6624**

13   Nielsen (18 September 2013), "'Binging' is the new viewing for over-the-top streamers", Nielsen newswire. **www.nielsen.com/us/en/newswire/2013/binging-is-the-new-viewing-for-over-the-top-streamers.html**

Of course, I don't even read half of them. You don't have to – it's not the point of Twitter. But this is a classic mistake in our thinking and highlights the problem of new technology adoption: it's treating the new medium just as if it were the old one.

To many, email is a bucket, a receptacle, into which information is deposited. In order to prevent it overflowing, you have to empty the bucket. And surely, they think, Twitter is the same. You're only using it correctly if you're reading everything, right?

The point is, *I'm not even sure that email is really like that.*

The time for buckets has passed. The torrent is too ferocious; the waters too high. We're up to our waists in it now and cannot expect to bail our way out.

CHEWING ON DATA'S EMPTY CALORIES

If we're not bingeing, we're still rarely consuming data in a way that aids digestion. The other great trap is to limit ourselves to snacking; you might even call it something positive-sounding like "information multi-tasking". But what's happening here is that quick "downloads" of content are replacing considered thought. And skipping from one app or website to the next threatens to overdose us with the inconsequential while we disregard the essential.

We are consuming the data equivalent of empty calories. Yes, we can chew on them for hours, but they don't satisfy our information needs.

Snacking itself is a relatively new development in food consumption. Although it began back in the 19th century, it is really a phenomenon of the 20th. Today, snacking has become the fourth meal of the day. On average we intake an additional 580 calories per day thanks to snacking – an astonishing additional 25% of our recommended daily intake.[14]

Interestingly, the world of work has played a significant part in this, whether it's how the structure of the working day in the Industrial Revolution shaped the established times for breakfast, lunch and dinner, through to today's working environment where the office is filled with an inescapable array of opportunities for a quick nutritional hit – in the office canteen, the coffee bar, or the inevitable and tempting tub of chocolates left out on someone's desk.

And just as the Industrial Revolution shaped how we consume food, so too has the knowledge revolution shaped how we consume information. Before the chocolate bar, nobody really ate between meals (although we did observe elevenses). Before the smartphone, nobody could really jump online in between sessions at the computer. The physical pounds have piled on, and now careless consumption of data is fattening our brains and making us unhealthy. We are suffering from "infobesity".

You could also call it a drug addiction – as mentioned earlier, it's all about dopamine, a neurotransmitter produced at the top of the brain stem that targets regions of the brain that control reward and movement.

---

14   Duffey, Kiyah J. and Popkin, Barry M. (28 June 2011), "Energy Density, Portion Size, and Eating Occasions: Contributions to Increased Energy Intake in the United States, 1977–2006", 10.1371, *PLOS Medicine* (San Francisco). **www.plosmedicine.org/article/ info%3Adoi%2F10.1371%2Fjournal.pmed.1001050**

'When we receive some valuable piece of information, or perform some act that promotes health and survival, such as eating, drinking, having sex, or making large amounts of money, dopamine is released along what are called the "pleasure pathways of the brain", providing us with rewarding, even euphoric, experiences. In fact our brain seems to value the dopamine more than the food, or drink, or sex, itself', says John Coates, a neuroscientist at the University of Cambridge and former Wall Street trader at Goldman Sachs, Merrill Lynch and Deutsche Bank.

FAILING TO COPE WITH INFORMATION EXCESS

Our destructive tendency to snack on information actually raises an interesting possibility. We can use this dopamine kick in clever ways – for example, through the gamification of work.

Gamification essentially takes the things that makes games rewarding and fun to play and uses them to encourage people towards certain actions or completing particular tasks in the real world. It might be as simple as awarding virtual badges to individuals who contribute the most to internal discussion forums or as complex as training people to adapt to new changes through entertaining yet educational software.

Could this help guide us though the digital deluge?

While gamification is highly effective, and can take the pain out of some tasks (it's a fantastic way of crowdsourcing the solutions to massive data problems, for instance), it can't be the only answer – not least because it has to send us down predetermined paths and therefore cannot support creativity.

Worse, it again supports the acquisition of the next quick hit rather than time spent reflecting and improving on the past one.

This simply compounds the problem we've already been discussing, creating stress, hampering clarity and ultimately degrading the performance of the individual. Whether we snack or binge – and whether we try to make a virtue of it or not through gamification – we are compounding the disconnect. We aren't getting any closer to the cognitive space we need to go deep and develop true knowledge and understanding.

Working in this way *doesn't* work. And it's already a problem around the world. A survey by LexisNexis of white-collar workers in the US, China, South Africa, UK and Australia suggests that people everywhere admit the quality of their work suffers at times because they can't sort through the information they need fast enough.[15] This in turn leads to behaviour that only makes the problem more acute.

Exasperated by the overwhelming volume of information, many managers fail to cope. They refuse to read long emails, reject long reports, and at their worst, blame others for their inability to summarise information adequately. But it's the manager and the employees who have *both* failed to identify the important information from the less so.

---

15   LexisNexis (20 October 2010), "New Survey Reveals Extent, Impact of Information Overload on Workers; From Boston to Beijing, Professionals Feel Overwhelmed, Demoralized". **www.lexisnexis.com/en-us/about-us/media/press-release.page?id=128751276114739**

Such a response just makes the problem worse. Individuals supplying the information get frustrated and further disconnected. It usually ends up with the manager possessing so little context that it becomes almost impossible to make the right decision. The cycle only spirals downward from there.

UNLOCKING THE POTENTIAL OF INFORMATION OVERLOAD

So if bingeing and snacking – and attempting to harness such habits – are non-starters, where does that leave us? They are the primary ways in which we've naturally responded to the information overload, and they haven't worked.

But they're not entirely dead-ends. In fact, you could say they're failed attempts at something that, done right, has worked before, and could work again. Because this is not the first information overload mankind has faced.

Since the invention of the printing press, society has actually always had access to more content than individuals could consume in a single lifetime. For hundreds of years we have been surrounded by a sea of content. The concept of being bewildered by the abundance of information is nothing unprecedented. The scale and immediacy of it has increased so phenomenally that it feels like something new; but it isn't.

What really matters is how we choose to navigate our way through it.

If we suffer from information overload, the real issue is what Clay Shirky calls 'filter failure' – essentially our own inability to see the wood for the trees.[16]

Getting this right is not just a technological problem – we can certainly develop better, faster and more customised algorithms – but it is also a question of improving the way in which we as humans discover, identify and consume information.

Snacking and bingeing are our first stabs at this filtration. They're primitive, instinctive – rapid-response survival techniques above all, and not great ones at that. If we carry on with them and other bad habits, we're not likely to make much progress.

It's similar to how we have started to replace our own memory with what *Wired*'s Clive Thompson called 'the perfect recall of silicon memory'.[17] On its own, this is OK if it's just a question of remembering random facts like who holds the world record for stuffing marshmallows up one single nostril (604, Toxteth O'Grady, USA) or the world's stickiest bogey (trick question, that's Toxteth again) but it's a critical failure if we deprive ourselves of the data points our brain needs to connect the dots and make the right connection.

The net effect of our inability to navigate through the digital deluge is that we deprive ourselves of the physical and mental space needed to generate ideas and innovation.

---

16   Doctorow, Cory (31 January 2010), "Clay Shirky on information overload versus filter failure", *Boing Boing*. **boingboing.net/2010/01/31/clay-shirky-on-infor**

17   Carr, Nicholas (July/August 2008), "Is Google Making Us Stupid?", *Atlantic Monthly* (Washington DC). **www.ncsl.org/print/racss/JRappaGoogle.pdf**

This is not a lament about cultural decline. The ability to go deep is a fundamental requirement for succeeding in the workplace. We deprive ourselves of the ability to succeed, and the world of business of the ability to compete.

But if we can find a way to filter the digital deluge, to identify the useful from the useless, we know that we can not only break bad habits – but also break new ground. We can start to harness rather than hide from the power that today's connectivity offers.

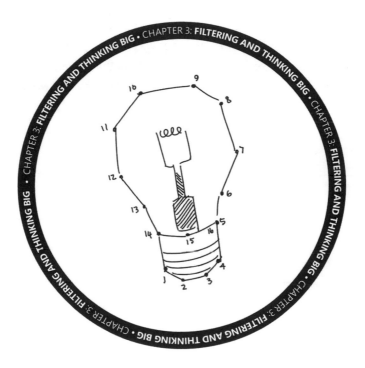

'Like many of the finest things in life, like happiness, tranquility and fame, the gain that was most precious was not the thing sought, but one that came of itself in the search for something else.'

– JUSTICE BENJAMIN N. CARDOZO

SO WHAT IS THE way forward? How can we embrace the chaos and beauty of our digital world – and its power?

As discussed in chapter 1, we are struggling to cope beneath a deluge of data and connectivity. If we don't push back, there will be few places left where we are undisturbed and have time to think: whilst asleep, perhaps, or in the shower. And given the trends of the Internet of Things and wearable technologies, I wouldn't count on those two vestiges of peace remaining all that long.

When it comes to how we respond, as we saw in chapter 2, it would be naive to assume that we can solve the problem by simply cutting down on the volume of information we access or by leaving ourselves at the mercy of our bingeing and snacking instincts.

So we need strategies and tools that help us better cope with information – and focus on what matters. But how do we sift through what's important and what's not? How do we decide when to tune in and when to tune out?

TUNING IN AND OUT

The good news is we have practice at tuning in and out already. We've actually been doing this for a long time – hundreds, if not thousands, of years. The content we consume has always already been winnowed by our own actions, admittedly often subconsciously.

Every time we make a choice about which newspaper to read, which radio station to listen to, which channel to watch and even which person to talk to, we are effectively establishing an information filter that will shape (and restrict) the content we receive.

It was just as true 30 years ago when we decided whether to read the *Times* or *Daily Mirror*. (Or in my case, to choose to escape reality altogether between the futuristic pages of *2000 AD*.)

All that's happened in the digital age, as the pool of data has grown, is that this process has gotten ever-more essential – and ever-more difficult.

But, at the same time, we've not been left unarmed against the task. The filters available to help us narrow our choices have multiplied; they've also been automated. Recommendation engines are constantly knife-and-forking their way through the internet to deliver increasingly personalised results based on what we've done in the past.

So the first thing to help us filter the flow is precisely that – filters (you can be fancy and call them "affinity-driven algorithmic recommendation engines" if you want; I don't mind). But since we already have them and are still up to our necks in the digital deluge, it's clear that in their current form they aren't enough.

As more and more data becomes available, it becomes obvious just how *basic* today's personalised services are. We've got a long way to go: being told that "people who have bought product A also bought product B" is not the most relevant or useful thing we can do. The data points are too few, the result too basic – and, as any grown adult who has been recommended a year's worth of Lego sets on the basis of buying a kid's birthday present one afternoon, half of the time it's just too clumsy.

So we need to be broadening our approach and integrating a whole range of data into these filters, and interpreting it much more thoughtfully and creatively. A good instance of a service already making progress in this area is Netflix, with its movie recommendations drawing on an increasingly rich variety of data to provide a personalisation experience based on way more than just which movies you have watched in the past. As we'll see again and again in this book, data has a lot of power like this that has scarcely been unlocked.

Social media also has a big role to play in making these filters more effective. The concept of trusted sources is far from new, but what this can mean for filtering in a data-soaked world has only begun to be explored.

Above all, trusting a source is a huge step in weeding out the signal from the noise – and social media should be perfect for that. This makes it one of the most important things to incorporate in more effective digital filters, though those of us with hundreds of "fake" friends (people we barely know rather than completely made-up individuals) are going to get less use out of it until we change our habits.

THE CREEPY VALLEY AND OVER-PERSONALISATION

So by integrating more data, as well as the insights of social media, filtering has a strong future in helping us outsmart the digital deluge. But, of course, the story isn't quite that simple. There are two pitfalls that come along with filtering and we need to consider them carefully if we're going to get things right.

The first is when things get, well, a bit icky.

After all, there's no reason the convenience of a filtered world can't reach some pretty eye-opening levels in the years ahead. Why couldn't the barkeeper of a bar we've never been to before greet us with our first name and favourite drink – a scenario described by Robert Scoble and Shel Israel, authors of *The Age of Context*? The technology is pretty much already in place to make it happen.

But if you just flinched at the thought of that, you're not alone. Welcome to the freaky factor of contextual computing. As we are the first generation of internet users, we are having to explore the boundaries of what's possible, what's sensible and what's acceptable. Some of my colleagues describe when things go too far as the 'creepy valley', where we're not quite sure of the value of what we're being offered and – more importantly – how the offer came to be made in the first place.

This needs to be seriously borne in mind. Next-generation filtering will fail if it doesn't feel helpful and natural, if it doesn't work with our expectations and only surprise us in pleasant ways; the better it gets, the greater the chance it can come up with some great but spooky (and ultimately unproductive) recommendations.

The second pitfall is closely related. As more and more of our digital experiences are personalised and tailored just for us, there is a risk of *over-personalisation* – a world that is full of filtered and "popular" content and devoid of genuine discovery, a place without happy accidents.

Essentially, it's a world in which you never quite know what you're missing because your favourite services have already decided that you don't want to see it.

Eli Pariser made great strides in establishing the debate over this in his book, *The Filter Bubble*. Here he exposed the dangers of a world where every element of data we receive is passed either openly or unobserved through a range of filters before we get it. Pariser also rightly praised the immense value of discoverability that filters can bring us – but ultimately, the risks of over-personalisation are too big to ignore. Taken to extremes, with everyone living in an over-personalised world, society will fragment and innovation cease.

HUMAN CONTROL

So surviving in the digital deluge requires filters – but not *just* smarter, more social ones. Crucially, for filtering to work, humans must take back control.

To begin with, in order to prevent filters streamlining the information we receive around preferences that are too narrow, we need to ensure that the filtering is *transparent*. In other words, we need to be able to recognise when decisions are being made for us. And then we need the control from those that provide such services to be able to fine-tune those choices. It's about being masters rather than slaves of data.

Even the most sophisticated, transparent and flexible filters have their limits, though, and these are particularly felt when we want to really expand and extend our thinking. If it feels impossible to connect the dots and think big when data is raging all around us, it's equally impossible when 99% of the data is – however helpfully and honestly – hidden from us.

So is this the end of thinking big? Not being able to unleash our full powers of innovation and truly make sense of it all would mean a rather hollow victory for next-generation filters, even if they can help us survive in the digital deluge. After all, we ultimately want to thrive in the digital deluge as well as survive.

Fortunately there could be a way out. And it lies in the origins of an unusual word from two and a half centuries ago.

SERENDIPITY AND THE IMPORTANCE OF DISCOVERY

Serendipity is one of those brilliant words the English language sometimes seems to specialise in. First used nearly 260 years ago, its etymology is a story in itself. Crucially it remains a word that is often used but rarely properly understood.

Today we talk of serendipity mostly in terms of a "happy accident", but this is only part of the tale. Its full meaning actually holds a key to true innovation and creativity.

The word was coined in England, but based on an ancient story from Persia that describes the adventures of the three princes of Serendip (modern-day Sri Lanka). This fairy tale travelled via 16th century Italy to England, where in 1754 it was brought into English through the letters of Horace Walpole. He used the term *serendipity* to describe the coming together of two elements that help attain wisdom: a happy accident, accompanied by the good judgement to know what to do with it.

The story tells of three princes, sent from their father's kingdom on a long journey to prepare them for succeeding him to the throne. Throughout they make discoveries that depend on both observation *and* wisdom. There are many stories of their travels, but the best-known is how they accurately describe a missing camel and its load without ever having seen the beast or its cargo. The runaway camel, they say, is half-blind, missing one front-left tooth, has a lame foot, and carries butter, honey and a pregnant woman.

The princes' detailed knowledge makes them seem suspicious, and they are held as thieves until the camel is found.

But for their insights, the brothers needed nothing more than "serendipity". As they were walking, they noticed a few things: the animal ahead of them had eaten grass on just one side of the road, even though it was much greener on the other (so it was probably blind on that side); the animal always dropped some grass on one side as it chewed (which hinted at a missing tooth); and the footprints showed that one of the animal's legs was being dragged (hence the lame foot). The creature was also losing some of its load: honey (sugar) had attracted flies, while butter (fat) had proven a draw for local ants.

As for the pregnant woman – well, I'm not even attempting to go there; let's just say that it involved a lot more checking of nearby pools of liquid than we would be prepared to do these days.

In a way, the brothers were ancient forerunners of Sherlock Holmes. Sir Arthur Conan Doyle would have been proud of their deductive reasoning. The clues were presented to them as a happy accident but it was their ability to work out what the clues meant that gave them the full benefit of serendipity.

So how can serendipity help us thrive in the age of the digital deluge? How can it unlock the power of innovation and creativity, both for individuals and organisations?

Firstly, we must make sure not to confuse the breadcrumb trail laid by recommendation engines with the materials for true serendipity. This trail is like following the instructions of a GPS device to get from A to B. It's of limited use for actual discovery. In an experiment by the University of Nottingham, people who followed the soothing voice of the GPS (*'take the second exit at the roundabout'*) were less able to sketch the route they had taken, understand their whereabouts and remember what they had seen than those who had used a map. The same is unfortunately true of anyone trying to think big by means of even the smartest filter.

Ultimately, the difference between thinking with a filter and thinking big with serendipity is like the difference between using a laser and a light bulb: the former will brightly illuminate a single point, while the latter will show us context and connections.

So to gain true insight, we need to find technology that – at the right time – switches from narrowing down on convenience to broadening out into opportunity. To connect the dots floating in the sea of digital information, we actually need to be able to see all the possible dots in the first place.

As Steven Johnson in his book *Where Good Ideas Come From* puts it, true innovation and creativity are rarely the outcome of one sudden eureka moment. Rather, they are the result of connectivity, of the piecing together of what he calls 'slow hunches', which collide, create sparks, and rub against each other until these borrowed and combined hunches and pieces of the puzzle come together and produce innovation.

The key word here is *connectivity*. The connections made and the ideas exchanged in London's coffee houses and the salons of Paris drove the Age of Enlightenment. Today, it is the internet and its marketplace of ideas that helps us to crowdsource innovation and tackle global problems.

The three princes of Serendip are now three billion people with a broadband connection.

As Steven Johnson puts it, yes, we're more distracted today, but we're also finding many more ways to connect, and can stumble serendipitously over new thoughts and insights and people like never before: 'chance favours the connected mind'.

JUDGING THE JUMP

Here's the rub: how do we know when to look for new slow hunches? When should we step away from the filters?

Ultimately I think it's going to be a bit like how we manage our body: we don't have to "think" to keep breathing. We probably don't even think too much as we walk home from the train station or the office; we're on autopilot. On the other hand, writing code, researching something in depth, working on a book is different.

We have to learn to make similar distinctions in our life in the digital deluge. And in the long run, I really do think it will come naturally. When it comes to moments that require convenience instead of a decision, why shouldn't we just use sophisticated algorithms and recommendation engines that factor in past choices and possible expectations? But when we need to make a significant mental leap, be it personal or work-related, we simply cannot rely on a source of information shaped entirely by filters. If we want to transform our current thinking, we must move beyond such boundaries.

The art is to find the right moment to step out of our comfort zone. The key is having software and culture that can help us once we do.

We've not mastered this yet, but with data increasingly abundant and accessible, it is obvious that we are edging closer to an age where we can set markers that will help us harness the flood of information and make sense of it all. Already breakthroughs are underway or impending in so many areas – as we'll see in the chapters ahead.

S O FAR IN THIS book, we've focused on exposing and responding to the problems created by the digital deluge, a world where technology risks disconnecting and distracting us, keeping us from performing to the best of our abilities both at work and at play.

But in the long run the digital deluge actually offers us more opportunities than it does threats, and this is as true for organisations as it is for individuals.

The challenge remains the same for both: how can they reorient themselves around the opportunities of a hyper-connected digital world? For organisations it's a world where their customers and employees are more connected and empowered than ever before.

Again, rather than trying to close the door on this or getting washed away entirely by surrendering without thought, the answer lies in using technology and a new generation of tools to harness the power of the digital deluge: helping firms to discover the next big insights or innovations that will transform their businesses in the digital age.

The beginning of this journey starts by uncovering the incredible value that already lies (often dormant) within most organisations: the value of their data.

MINING THE DATA DIVIDEND

Let's step back for a moment. Do we all appreciate how dramatically our shopping habits have changed?

Twenty years ago, we didn't enter shops with reams of detailed spec sheets, surveys of previous customers and notebooks full of rumours and pointed questions tucked up under our arms. When we spotted a deal on a shelf, we didn't have a small suitcase of magazine and newspaper cuttings trundling along in a suitcase behind us that we could quickly consult for the critical lowdown. If we fancied a shirt or a pair of shoes, we didn't snap a picture, head to the chemists to get it developed and then share it with friends and family for their feedback before deciding to buy. When a book looked great but a bit pricey, we didn't write down its ISBN and use the store phone to ring up and see whether it was cheaper elsewhere. And we didn't do the majority of our Christmas shopping from our sofa.

Hardly any of the goods or services we bought were truly virtual. When we needed inspiration, we went window-shopping or looked through a catalogue instead of browsing what our neighbours had stuck on their cork-boards or photo albums. And when we were unhappy with a company's service, we probably called, wrote a letter, or maybe sent an email – but we didn't go out into the street and announce our displeasure to the passing public.

Today, one device in our pocket let's us do all of the above and more, with the use of about four apps. Have organisations really responded to this as much as they should – and can?

Technology has transformed the relationship between customers and companies; the concept of customer loyalty has entirely new parameters. We even have an ugly buzzword for it: the omnichannel consumer.

For my part, I prefer to speak of the *connected customer*,[18] because the real change is not so much where people shop, but about the context in which they shop – and crucially, this context is driven by data.

---

18   Brian Solis at Altimeter Group calls it the 'connected customer'. Solis, Brian (9 April 2012), "Meet Generation C: The Connected Customer". **www.briansolis.com/2012/04/meet-generation-c-the-connected-customer**

DATANOMICS

Today's customers don't make key buying decisions merely based on clever advertising (although it clearly still helps, just ask the Meerkat).[19] Instead, they use a blend of signals to make their choice. They demand a dialogue.[20] They want companies to meet them on their own terms, and on their territory, wherever they happen to be. And they listen to those around them who they trust – in a social media world you are never more than two clicks away from your friend or family's recommendation.

Of course, it goes much deeper than that. The instant responses of today's always-on world have led customers to expect an always-on, anytime, anywhere service. And crucially, more and more often such services don't involve the exchange of money, but data.

It's a quid-pro-quo: companies offer free or cheaper services in return for the monetisable data trail left by their customers. It is a symbiosis, as mutually beneficial as that between Nemo the clownfish and his sea anemone.

Many companies are only slowly beginning to understand the inherent value of such data exchanges. Others have already built their entire business model around them – from Facebook and Twitter to Amazon and Google.

From a company's point of view, it's an exercise in data-mining and analysis: illuminating the dark data of what's happening

---

19   **youtu.be/M0mXUC0cUPg**

20   Petro, Greg (14 March 2013), "Retailer Customer Relationships – Who Defines Who?", *Forbes* (New York). **www.forbes.com/sites/gregpetro/2013/03/14/retailer-customer-relationships-who-defines-who**

on the shop floor (whether that's a website or a physical store) and turning it into deep insight that helps it understand its customers and anticipate their needs.

However, most companies are still trying to understand what's really changed in the relationship with their customers. As we will discuss later, this is because most businesses are stuck thinking only about a very narrow dimension of this relationship – the actual transaction itself.

They are struggling to figure out how the insight provided by data has the potential of reinstating or reinventing a retailer's historical relationship with the customer – which was lost when we started to abandon the local store with its narrow choice and began to shop around.

So instead of fighting against the data onslaught, how can organisations harness the digital deluge to transform the customer experience? To start with, they need to completely redefine their expectations of customers to be more reflective of the potential offered by a digital world. Instead of the narrow lens of "current transaction" they need to connect the disparate dots of data to form a holistic, "multi-dimensional" view of the people who will ultimately become responsible for their success (or failure).

Let me use a personal example to demonstrate.

THE MULTI-DIMENSIONAL CUSTOMER

A few months ago, I made an appointment to take my motorbike to my regular dealer for a set of new tyres.

I dropped in to the dealership on my way into work; I had a quiet morning of paperwork (email) and a busy afternoon of meetings ahead. As I dropped off the keys to the service representative I told them I'd need to leave in an hour or so due to that afternoon's commitments. Not a problem, I was told; it was only a couple of tyres and they had been expecting me.

Unfortunately, it wasn't until three and a half hours later that I was finally able to leave.

Don't mistake this as a rant against the motorcycle dealer. I could have vented my spleen and pulled the "social" trigger in a fit of pique long ago, but I didn't. It's perhaps a sad statement on the motorcycle-servicing industry, but this dealer is actually almost as good as it gets.

The point of this story is that what actually happened wasn't really poor customer service. It was poor customer experience. They provided a perfectly friendly and technically competent service that nevertheless completely mis-matched my expectations and needs simply by being blind to the information they had at their disposal and unable to adapt their processes accordingly.

By the time I had finally been handed back my keys, I had been given four key statements as to the delay:

1. 'Sorry you've had to wait, but it's really busy in the workshop today.'

2. 'Sorry it took so long, the mechanic is new and has come from a dealership of a different brand of motorcycle and is not yet familiar with these machines.'

3. 'Thanks for your patience, but we've run a full safety check on your vehicle and it looks like everything is OK except you might need new brake pads in another 4,000 miles.'

4. 'Sorry for the delay, the bike's now ready but it's just off being washed. It will just be another 20 minutes.'

What had gone wrong? Some of the problems were arguably unavoidable – a rush in their workshop, for instance, could have been down to outside influences – but a huge number were self-inflicted and unnecessary. Did I really need the bike cleaned if I was now more than two hours past the time we'd first established as being vital for my departure?

That was a nice big, juicy bit of data that I had offered up to them on a plate, and it went missing almost straightaway when it came to delivering the service I paid for.

The point of this pretty basic example is that organisations of every kind are failing to tailor their services to a huge number of data points offered up by their customers – some every bit as huge and obvious as mine, some subtle and sophisticated, all increasing in number almost every day (online *and* offline). Paying attention to them is vital if firms are going to successfully compete for customers in the future.

Put simply, the bike dealership failed to see me as a "connected customer". Understanding the potential of the connected customer is about opening organisations up to the fact that their customers are not one-dimensional, and information on their needs and expectations not only exist but are increasingly accessible.

This is where the data-soaked, hyper-connected nature of the digital deluge is very much our friend – if we can take advantage of what it offers.

THE FOUR DIMENSIONS OF THE CONNECTED CUSTOMER

There are four key dimensions that comprise today's connected customer and each of these need to be factored into an organisation's approach to customer service in order to provide a customer experience worthy of the digital age.

The first is pretty standard and is something organisations have focused on for hundreds of years. It's simply the dimension of "current" context. Put simply, it's focusing on the single transaction that has led me inside the shop or to an organisation's website – it's the basic question of "what is it I'm here to do today?" Be it buy a television, get car insurance or new tyres for my motorcycle.

The second dimension brings in the "historical" context of my previous transactions. This is a dimension that has grown in prominence with the advance of online shopping and is reflected by the sort of service that says 'Welcome back Dave, in the past you've bought this, would you like another one or perhaps something related?'

For my motorcycle tyre example, this could be as simple as looking back through my customer history to see what my last transactions were. Has the bike been recently serviced?

What information was the customer offered previously? And so on. What the dealership actually already knew was that they had serviced my bike two months and 2,000 miles ago and had already advised me I would need new brake pads in about 6,000 miles.

But in addition to the basic historical analysis of completed transactions, we need to extend this definition of history to include incomplete transactions too. The boundary between my digital and analogue worlds needs to be knocked down by combining the relevant information I have previously been looking at online with a real-life service that builds on it, not ignores it.

The final two additional dimensions paradoxically offer the greatest opportunity and the greatest challenge.

The third dimension is to understand the customer as a "holistic" individual. As human beings, our identities are incredibly complex and nuanced. A recent UK government report on the future of identity goes a long way to articulating this.[21] It shows that as individuals we exhibit several different identities or personas throughout the day depending on the context of where we are, what we're doing and how we feel.

Organisations that can reach out and understand more about these personas will be able to recognise the primary persona being used for a transaction. They will then be able to blend that with the second dimension to deliver a service that is truly reflective of the entirety of who they're dealing with.

---

21   Government Office for Science (21 January 2013), "Future identities: changing identities in the UK". **www.bis.gov.uk/assets/foresight/docs/identity/13-523-future-identities-changing-identities-report.pdf**

In my example I had openly declared at least two different personas when I entered the showroom – dressed like I was, I was obviously a motorcyclist, but I also revealed I had a job (which paid for the bike and fancy fluorescent gear) and that I needed to get that done too.

The fourth and final dimension is a "social" one and it's about understanding both the incoming and outgoing potential that my connection to other people offers. This is more than just "twhining" (complaining incessantly over Twitter). It's about realising that I am part of a connected social network and therefore could exert significant damage (or praise) when I talk openly about a brand I've come into contact with.

Don't laugh this off as a petty threat. Done properly, this can have significant impact. Ask United Airlines – they know. Canadian musician Dave Carroll's "United Break Guitars" – a song describing the airline's jaw-dropping mistreatment of his $3,500 Taylor guitar – promptly went viral in 2009, causing more damage than even a United baggage handler could dream of.[22]

More importantly, this fourth dimension can be a much more positive force. It offers incredible insights if you use it to understand the people a customer is really connected with. This is about using the customer's "social graph" to help understand them better, just as a whole new generation of advertisers and service providers are finding through Facebook. The power of the social graph is that it offers the potential to offer me something extra by tapping into my

---

22   Hammond, Joshua (16 July 2009), "United Airlines and consumer generated turbulence", *Nielsen Online*. **www.nielsen.com/us/en/newswire/2009/united-airlines-and-consumer-generated-turbulence.html**

"trusted network" – this only really works for my real friends (not the 700 fake ones I have to impress people with) but it allows me to use a human element (trust) to help me make my decision or to judge the results. Being recommended a product or service by someone I actually know is much more useful than being told the same by a stranger because knowing the individual I can validate the credibility of the comment.

So back to my beloved motorcycle dealer. They just didn't realise that they had all this information at hand and, worse still, even if they did realise they had it they simply couldn't adjust their processes to accommodate it. *I process, therefore I am.* The ability to adapt internal processes and transcend established organisational boundaries is probably *the* most crucial problem facing organisations seeking to provide great customer service in a connected world.

But it's not just the disconnected organisation that will present the challenge. Much of the problem in living up to the potential of the four-dimensional customer lies in the fact that the data required to build this holistic view is itself completely disparate. It lies in completely different places inside and outside of the organisation, is unstructured and unintelligible in its raw form.

In order to be able to stitch it all together and provide meaningful insight, we're going to need a new generation of customer relationship management tools that can transcend the internal/external boundaries of the organisation, connecting to disparate data sets and turning them into a common, natural language or representation that can be acted upon in real-time by individuals and organisations. We may not be there yet, but organisations are increasingly realising that CRM is going to become so much more than just better intelligence on the organisation's internal data.

The real irony here is that the digital deluge actually offers the solution, but only if the organisations and the individuals within can reorient themselves to take advantage of it.

THE END OF ORGANISATIONAL SILOS

Of course, too many companies don't seem to get it – yet. They fail to open themselves up to the customer, ignore the vast data that is available to them and instead appear dysfunctional, operating within their own corporate silos. They focus on the process rather than the customer outcome.

Connected customers, however, are highly demanding. They expect companies to meet their every need, with the same reliability as a click on a web link. To these consumers, 'any obstacle between you and what you seek is unacceptable. Loyalty goes to companies that support you in those demands, while you'll dump the others in a heartbeat if there's a more connected alternative', says Josh Bernoff, senior vice president at Forrester Research.[23]

To succeed, companies have to raise their game, make sure they create positive feedback loops that create real value for their customers – through connections, through knowledge and data insight, through the serendipity of discovery, and through services and incentives.[24]

---

23   **youtu.be/Atp9ibcofaM**

24   Blase, Paul and Rao, Anand (9 December 2013), "Information as an asset", *Financial Times*. **www.ft.com/cms/s/0/0919f8b2-6105-11e3-b7f1-00144feabdc0.html**

Companies have to factor this in, because – as a study by consulting firm Accenture shows – consumers now actively research buying decisions in a way that is crowding out the traditional sources of information and marketing. More importantly, today's connected customers are starting to understand the power that comes from harnessing the digital deluge by actively using channels of information that give them a choice, that offer a dialogue.[25]

But that's just the first step, a hint of what the future holds for the connected customer. What's really emerging is what the US hacker Josh Klein calls 'reputation economics',[26] with emerging technologies and social software driving the economic value and status of the consumer in a way that takes the symbiotic relationship between the connected customer and the supplier to an entirely new level.

Before we all climb to the lofty heights of reputation economics, we also have to overcome a few obstacles first. And we will only manage to do that if customers and companies come together – by agreeing on the tools and ground rules to make it happen.

Because if they don't, both sides will simply stare at each other across the abyss of creepy valley, where neither is sure what information should be used and how. As data becomes an ever-more-valuable asset (probably the most valuable asset that a company can hold), customers will only surrender this

25   Accenture (2013), "The Connected Consumer is Here".
www.accenture.com/Microsites/changingconsumer/Documents/pdf/Accenture-Video-Transcript-Connected-Consumer.pdf

26   Klein, Joshua (November 2013), *Reputation Economics: Why Who You Know is Worth More Than What You Have* (Palgrave Macmillan, New York). **www.reputation-economics.com**

information in return for transparent service that delivers tangible value.

Ultimately, transformational customer service requires transformed organisations. Organisations need to stop thinking about their own silos, structure and processes because the customer simply doesn't (and shouldn't) care. When you advertised your product, you didn't advertise the complexities of your organisational structure or the processes you have adopted or been forced to use. It's time we finally put an end to the cry of "I'm sorry, but that's not my department", because increasingly it's just a strong signal of a company that is failing to adapt to the new connected world.

And underneath all of this is the simple misunderstanding that having too much data is a barrier rather than an opportunity. Organisations that learn how to unleash the power of data for both their customers and their employees will be the ones that make the most of this new world.

And the secrets of becoming an organisation like this – where the digital deluge is no longer feared but taken advantage of – are the subject of the next chapter.

Case study: Ted Baker

BRITISH FASHION DESIGN house and lifestyle brand Ted Baker has already begun to harness the value of the data that lies within its organisation in order to give customers the experience they want.

Ted Baker was created in 1988 as a specialist shirt shop and today has 362 stores and concessions around the world in countries including Turkey, China and Australia, as well as the UK. The company has access to huge volumes of customer data. Using this creatively forms a central part of its strategy for growth over the next 10–15 years. As the volume of customer information increases, the company is well-positioned to further increase the value of its own data dividend, enhancing customer experience to suit changing tastes and preferences.

Head of finance, Charles Anderson, says that 'the key benefit to gathering large volumes of data is that we have been able to link all of the data together and then most importantly decipher what to do with it'.

The company culture clearly supports this approach. The customer is truly at the heart of Ted Baker's business model; it doesn't work in silos and regardless of whether it's the retail business, the wholesale business, or the e-commerce business, the firm strives to use technology to ensure that 'the customer is always at the centre'.

By using technology intelligently and harnessing insights gained from its own digital deluge, Ted Baker is at the forefront of making each customer journey connected, seamless and unique. Anderson continues: 'We do a lot already with customer data, we are trying to understand who our customer is and we are trying to be clever with things…How do we make that customer journey wherever they shop with us? How do we harness that information? One of the real benefits that [software] will give us is linking all of that data together and then figuring out what we do with that data.'

The numbers add up as well. The company has made great strides over the past year, recording pre-tax profits of £40 million and website sales up 55%. By listening to its customers and connecting those insights – by joining and then harnessing disparate sources of digital data – Ted Baker has the ability to anticipate and embrace change as well as support future global expansion.

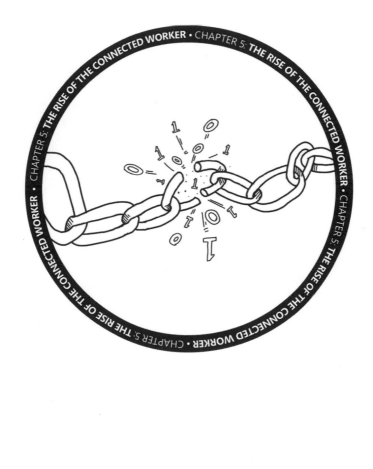

CHAPTER 5: THE RISE OF THE CONNECTED WORKER • CHAPTER 5: THE RISE OF THE CONNECTED WORKER • CHAPTER 5: THE RISE OF THE CONNECTED WORKER • CHAPTER 5: THE RISE OF THE CONNECTED WORKER

UNLEASHING THE WORKFORCE

ONE OF THE MOST exciting aspects of the future of work is unlocking the incredible potential we as individuals can bring to our organisations. This is a hugely rewarding development for all involved – something increasingly forced on firms by the digital deluge, but which will also pay incredible dividends if it's handled correctly.

I know it sounds blindingly obvious, but for many years the fullness of what we can offer our employers has often lain hidden and untapped, sometimes by accident, sometimes because our organisations simply either didn't know how (or worse, didn't want) to access and harness it.

And the reasons are obvious: too many companies are hierarchical; they rely on command and control; they trap data in silos; fearing the digital deluge, they restrict information flows and trickle information only to the top – as if that were the only place to find knowledge and insight. Given dramatic advances in technology, it's baffled me for quite some time now why we still organise our workplaces the way the Egyptians built the pyramids.

Such companies are not fit for the emerging Big Data economy: they will either drown in data, be blind to their customers, or lose out to competitors.

Going by the majority of the feedback to *Business Reimagined*, it seems that book struck a chord with employers and employees both searching for a way to prevent this. Increasingly they are doing so by finding better ways for people in organisations to be engaged and empowered.

The main hook for the opening of that book was a damning statement from a US survey that showed that a huge proportion (71%) of the American workforce were disengaged at work. It remains a frightening statistic that we see repeated again and again around the world.

However, what I didn't do at the time was dive into more detail about why the lack of engagement is so problematic for organisations, not just in terms of what it means to employers today, but more importantly what it will mean to them tomorrow.

There are some pretty obvious statements to make – "happy workers make happy customers" being just one of them – but in reality the connection is much more significant, complex and altogether more powerful.

TRANSFORMATIONAL EMPLOYEES

A few months ago, I found myself sat in an office talking to the chief marketing officer for one of the world's largest retailers. We were discussing many things about the future of retail, about blurring the digital/analogue boundary, the multi-dimensional customer and so on.

After a while the CMO stopped me in my tracks and said simply: 'Look Dave, I'm responsible for delivering a transformational customer experience. And I know that in order to do that I need engaged employees who are empowered with the right tools, data and culture in order to be transformational.'

Wow! He said in one sentence what I had failed to say in an entire book. The simplicity of the connection within that sentence has haunted me ever since; it perfectly captures the challenge and opportunity that the digital deluge offers every organisation.

First of all, here at last is the brutal recognition that none of this matters if employees aren't empowered to deliver a service required (or expected) by customers. You can throw as much technology and process as you like at this problem and the outcome will always remain the same – you *will* fail.

That doesn't mean to say that the technology and process aren't important (and I say that not just because I've still got my own bills to pay). But it's that they are secondary or supportive to the massive *cultural* change that is required in order for individuals to be able to unleash their potential and for their organisation to be able to harness it.

Secondly, it recognises that old adage that the power of a company is defined by the cumulative power of its people.

As explored in *Business Reimagined*, the way in which most organisations have sought to harness this power is more reflective of the much more straightforward, hierarchical approach that was the norm of our pre-internet society.

But now, things are different. The flat, seemingly chaotic, connected nature of the web is having a direct impact on our society both in terms of how we access, acquire and share information, and in what this means for our own expectations about how and where we contribute to all aspects of our lives. Through things like social media, the digital deluge is teaching us that it's good to share and that great things can happen when we do. Unfortunately, it's now our inability to change from the historical hierarchy of work culture that's holding us back.

But the rise of the connected worker is already underway – and the firms that don't unleash their employees will be the ones that get left behind.

OPENING UP THE INTERNAL SERENDIPITY ECONOMY

The opportunity of getting this right for organisations extends way beyond simple competitive advantage. We are in dire need of what Daniel Rasmus calls the 'serendipity economy',[27] with technology that connects people and data, releases their spontaneity and drives innovation.[28]

The value of such internal information marketplaces, of course, is not just the ability to follow a company's internal flow of consciousness, but the fact that they are searchable archives of best practice. According to the McKinsey Global Institute, internal social networks can become the publication of record for a company's expertise and knowledge – cutting by 35% the time staff usually spend on tracking down business information.[29]

The return on investment here is not just obvious benefits like higher customer satisfaction and profitability. Connecting workers to sidestep hierarchies is also becoming an important tool for employee retention. Rasmus points to the case of a young staffer at accountants Deloitte in Australia, who did not get frustrated with corporate bureaucracy because he could

27   Rasmus, Daniel W. (2011), "Welcome to the Serendipity Economy". **danielwrasmus.com/wp-content/uploads/Rasmus-WelcometotheSerendipityEconomy.pdf**

28   Rasmus, Daniel W. (20 August 2013), "The Serendipity Economy: How Spontaneity Plus Social Networking Drives Innovation", *Fast Company*. **www.fastcompany.com/3015886/leadership-now/the-serendipity-economy-how-spontaneity-plus-social-networking-drives-innovat**

29   Chui, Michael; Manyika, James; Bughin, Jacques; Dobbs, Richard; Roxburgh, Charles; Sarrazin, Hugo; Sands, Geoffrey; Westergren, Magdalena (July 2012), "The social economy: Unlocking value and productivity through social technologies", Report (McKinsey Global Institute).
www.mckinsey.com/insights/high_tech_telecoms_internet/the_social_economy

use an internal social network to convince senior partners of a great idea, which had an immediate positive impact on customers.

As we transition to this new data-empowered world where the digital deluge is celebrated not feared, these social shortcuts are the tools for a perfect symbiosis – combining the technical and social media knowledge of young digital natives with the strategic understanding of more senior colleagues.[30]

Are enterprise social networks alone the panacea? Of course not! Might they have helped speed up the development of the poster boy of slow-starting ideas, 3M's Post-It note, which suffered more than five years of rejection before it caught on?[31] Most likely!

The potential for change is dramatic. The McKinsey Global Institute recently put its finger in the wind and estimated that the 'second generation of IT Consumerisation'[32] (adopting the principles that make social media work so well in our personal lives to change the culture of collaboration inside organisations) could unlock $1.3 trillion worth of value from companies, through increased efficiency of workers who can deal faster with workflow and problems.[33]

---

30   Kane, Gerald C. (18 July 2013), "Procedural Versus Strategic Approaches to Social Media", *MIT Sloan Management Review* blog. **sloanreview.mit.edu/article/procedural-versus-strategic-approaches-to-social-media**

31   Hiskey, Daven (9 November 2011), "Post-It notes were invented by accident", *Today I Found Out.* **www.todayifoundout.com/index.php/2011/11/post-it-notes-were-invented-by-accident**

32   We discussed this in more detail in *Business Reimagined*, pp.51–2.

33   Kane, Gerald C. (21 August 2013), "Social Business: Flat or Hierarchical? A Surprising Answer", *MIT Sloan Management Review* blog. **sloanreview.mit.edu/article/social-business-flat-or-hierarchical-a-surprising-answer**

CULTURE, CULTURE, CULTURE

Studies show that technology barriers are only partly to blame for the lack of collaboration. Company culture and management structures are much bigger hurdles. But here's where the benefit of technology and the digital deluge come into play: introducing new tools in a company that seek to unleash the power of the digital deluge forces the business to rethink itself, and to make that quantum leap that empowers the connected worker.

But the information revolution in business will go much further. And to understand where we are heading, we first have to understand the difference between data and information.

For us computer folks, data is the raw stuff: numbers and facts, structured and unstructured, collected everywhere and anywhere – from your email inbox to your company's web server logs, from traffic flow measurements and phone conversations to online search queries and mobile phone location data. Many companies ignore data; they treat it like stuff in the attic, and its true value remains hidden (a bit like an old Bitcoin wallet in some arcane folder structure lost on a creaking hard drive). In these companies, data remains dark data. Very valuable, but not a lot of people in the company know that it exists or where to find it.

So what's information, then? Well, this most precious of commodities is what we get once the data has been processed. When we have queried the data to extract some meaning – and I'll discuss in the next chapter where we might be heading there.

For companies, though, it is not enough to turn the data into information; to make it work, they have to share this information with their workers (and arguably with their business partners), because in most cases only those with immediate experience at the corporate coalface will actually understand the information and turn it into deep insight.

Paradoxically, in order to succeed, organisations need to be confident enough to make the "problem" worse. They need to embrace and extend the digital deluge within their organisations by breaking down the information silos and providing access to more and more information for all their employees. Yes, that risks soaking individuals with a seemingly endless information-firehose, but if those individuals are equipped with the right tools, and crucially, empowered with the right culture, they will soon demonstrate the transformative power it represents.

Once again, it is the humans who hold the key to our success, and organisations need to ensure that they are doing all that they can to create an environment that generates and supports new skills that will lead to future success.

THE NEW ALCHEMISTS

Many years ago, a friend of mine once lovingly referred to me as a 'technology alchemist'. He was politely making fun of me, of course, because a) he knew that the "precious metal" of the solution I was describing at the time was made from worthless ingredients and b) more importantly, I was simply waxing lyrical about a solution that would require "magic" to work and therefore would ultimately prove to be impossible.

Frustratingly, back then, he was probably right.

For all the truth of his well-meaning character assassination it is a phrase that has stuck with me (and my CV) ever since. Several years later, I had the incredible opportunity to share a platform with the great (and wonderfully inspiring) Charles Handy who, back in 1999 (while I was still wandering around in short hair), was using the concept of alchemy to describe the essential characteristics of entrepreneurs.

In his eyes, start-up high-flyers were strikingly similar to the alchemists of old.

Although Handy's focus remained primarily on individuals operating outside of organisations, his focus on the core characteristics of alchemists is particularly helpful. The concepts of dedication, doggedness and difference are as valuable to creative individuals working *within* organisations as they are to individuals working outside them.

I believe that within every individual inside an organisation lies an "intrapreneur" – a part of them with an innate desire to make things better, either directly for themselves or indirectly by making their organisation better. Our main cultural challenge is how organisations not only create an environment that supports this, but equally how they learn to live with the occasional chaos that can come with it.

But what I really want to emphasise is that creating an environment for intrapreneurship is far more than simply defining a *process* for it. The process itself is worthless if neither the individuals nor the organisation know what to do with it. Without addressing that you simply create the modern-day canteen suggestion box – unloved and ultimately unused by either employee or employer.

TIME FOR A NEW "CAREER"

Thankfully, the challenges of the economy and the opportunities of the digital age have begun to drive a similarly profound change in many employers' attitudes. They know they need innovation from within – and thanks to the experience we all have with the digital deluge (both positive and negative) we are all elevating our expectations of what technology can make possible for us. Whilst there is still some occasional reluctance, the doors are fundamentally more open now than they've ever been.

And it's in the *aspirations* of individuals that perhaps the most significant change has taken place. The digital deluge has fundamentally changed our hopes and ambitions, from the incredible experiences of what technology can accomplish in our personal lives, right through to the ability to learn about almost any topic imaginable with a ridiculously low barrier to entry (access to a computer and the internet rather than high fees or previous academic achievements).

This has resulted in individuals becoming more and more aware of their full potential – not just for their current employer, but for themselves as a whole. The challenge now is how do organisations and individuals come together within this context to build a new relationship that is more representative and better placed to take advantage of our potential in the digital age?

Here, too, Handy offers sage counsel. His long-standing concept of the "portfolio career" is becoming both possible and normal, something accessible to us mere humans as well as high-flyers.

Handy's solution is for individuals to focus on the five elements of their own portfolio career throughout their lives. This concept is notable for many reasons, but the primary thrust is that the term "career" is no longer formed around a single industry or even vocation as it was in my father's day. Instead, it should be formed around the individual as a holistic human being (sound familiar?).

According to Handy, the five elements your portfolio should include are:

- paid work (your day job)

- fee work (something you do to provide specific products or services like bake cupcakes or provide consultancy to a local social enterprise)

- gift work (what you do for your community or charity)

- home work (what you invest in your family)

- and finally, study work (always, always be learning).

What's happened is that against the backdrop of changes in society, the digital deluge has brought individuals the awareness and opportunity to do things differently.

Organisations are increasingly realising this too – understanding that an engaged, vibrant yet mildly chaotic workforce is far better than a permanent but predictable one. Sounds like how a start-up might behave? Precisely my point. Whether they are nimble challengers or corporate giants, companies have to organise themselves differently.

It is a time for intelligent organisms rather than organisations.

UNBOXING THE INBOX

So when it comes to the connected worker, companies need to "unbox" their employees – to unleash them, to let them break free. Give them the tools they need to make discoveries; foster a culture of constant iteration and innovation; cut through the hierarchies. And most of all, help them harness the power of the digital deluge. Help them cultivate all aspects of their own portfolio careers and then look beyond the boundaries of their defined roles so that all that they offer can benefit the organisation: bringing new and sometimes unexpected opportunities, wisdom and experience.

For many, it won't be easy to make the transition. Yet again, we encounter the "first-generation" hurdle. Instead of shovelling through our inboxes or mining narrow sets of company data, we have to learn how to use computing power to first identify the dots of our working and personal lives and then learn to connect them as well.

Data and information tools give us the power to reach well beyond the boundaries of the corporations we work for. And here I want to doff my cap to the enterprising software developer in the United States who, without telling his employer, outsourced the tasks he was employed to fulfil to China and spent his workdays surfing the internet.[34]

---

34 www.bbc.co.uk/news/technology-21043693

I'm not saying for a minute that this was a smart thing to do, but there is part of me that thinks that with the right culture and the right framework then maybe there is more merit in this than simply being able to "bunk off". If we have the tools to work more efficiently, and then spend our working days to do something that's – hopefully – more meaningful, isn't that something to strive for?

Companies are only beginning to learn how technology can help them to unleash their staff, while workers are only beginning to understand how the digital deluge can mean open, transparent access to information that gives them true power to make a difference.

All we have to do now is learn the ground rules, and develop the tools to make it work.

Case study: Delta Airlines

LEADING AMERICAN AIRLINE, Delta, understands that in order to deliver a transformational customer experience it needs engaged employees empowered with the right tools, information and culture. To get to that point, it has quickly transitioned to a technology-first business.

The company's overhaul had a two-pronged approach. Firstly, Delta wanted to equip its pilots with state-of-the-art mobile technology to reduce the huge volume of paper in the cockpit. Deploying tablet devices across the entire fleet meant that the carrier could remove traditional pilot flight bags maintained on board aircraft for each pilot (weighing in at a hefty 17Kg each). That critical weight reduction is expected to reduce fuel consumption by an estimated 1.2 million gallons per year, which translates to almost 12 million kilogrammes of reduction in carbon emissions – the equivalent of taking more than 2,500 passenger cars off the road.

As Delta had already implemented WiFi across its fleet, the next step was to add to its customer experience. So the second huge shift that Delta made was to get rid of the traditional point-of-sale systems flight attendants carried during the flight for refreshments or duty free and replace them with smartphones.

And while the dramatic reduction in paperwork and fuel costs (estimated at around $13m) of these changes is reason enough to make them happen in any organisation, the real benefit is actually yet to be felt, for it is the *cultural* dividend of empowering every member of the flight crew with a connected device that will ultimately change things most.

Already it has had a noticeable positive impact on the pilots. Captain Steve Dickson, Delta's senior vice president of flight operations, says that 'by eliminating paper, we reduce clutter and minimise time spent looking for flight information, allowing our pilots the opportunity for greater situational awareness in the air and on the ground'.

And 19,000 flight attendants are now empowered to engage and react real-time in the provision of the best service for their customers, regardless of whether they are in-flight or on the ground.

They're no longer confined by antiquated systems to selling snacks and drinks, but set free by flexible technology to, say, help customers find ground transportation and departure gates, or check their own work schedules to increase efficiency. The future of this kind of connected service for a world of connected customers is immense.

Delta has reaped the rewards from a visionary shift in its approach to both customer and employee engagement, and there is no reason why any business, no matter how big or small, can't do the same.

THE BIG DATA BANDWAGON

BIG DATA EH? I know, I know, it's one of the biggest bandwagons in the world of technology, but even I am not exempt from succumbing to the charm of what a Big Data world might bring.

Still, the word "big" is silly; data has no concept of size, be it big or small. We might as well call it "humongous", "yellow" or "fluffy" data for all it means to statisticians. But here's what's more worrying: most people and organisations have absurdly low expectations of what Big Data can actually do for us.

We're so busy worrying about the digital deluge that we've started to downplay the potential of what having more and more information actually makes possible. Instead of looking up to that potential, we start to narrow down the scope, talking not of transformation but of "insight" and "analysis" instead. To me, describing Big Data as a form of "business insight" or "business intelligence" is a bit like describing the modern computer as a "really good calculator". Frankly, we need to set our sights much higher.

So let me suggest where we should start: Big Data and the insight we'll gain from it will fundamentally change what it means to be human. There, I said it.

Yes, it sounds ridiculous, but there's a truly seismic change ahead, just as big as when Pythagoras and Parmenides, in the 6th and 5th century (BC), used data to prove the earth was spherical not flat; when Copernicus, in the 16th century, used data to show it was the sun not the earth at the centre of our universe; and when Darwin, in 1859, used the power of data to explain evolution as the real origin of species.

Significantly, the new world of data doesn't just result in change that will shake the foundations of most of our existing knowledge; it will also turn the very premise of how we approach science, economics and business theory on its head as well.

CORRELATION VS CAUSALITY

What Pythagoras, Parmenides, Copernicus and Darwin (and every scientist before and after them) had in common is this: they had access to a small amount of data, and used a heap of (incredibly smart) theory to fill in the blanks. The world of science is a world of causality and cogitation.

In a true Big Data world we go way beyond that, because here the sample size *"n"* is no longer a subset of the overall potential statistical population; instead it is the *entire* statistical population.

A Big Data world is a world where *n=all*.

However, as our sample set approaches *n=all*, (and our tools to understand the sample become ever more powerful), our scientific approach changes. With access to a huge amount of fact, we have to theorise less. The digital deluge will inevitably mean that the data will speak for itself.

In this Big Data world, it is correlation not causality that becomes king. To some extent the *what* becomes more important than the *why*.

Until now, scientists had to look for causality; they lacked the data (with the means to capture, store or analyse) to do anything other than theorise why certain things might happen, e.g. *A* happens, therefore *B* occurs. And if you also change *C*, we get a completely new chain of causality.

But there's an obvious problem with proving such causalities. To understand our world:

- we can either look at a small but fairly up-to-date set of data points (for example, a survey with a small sample size)

- or we can try to capture all data points – but that is both costly and slow. As the chief executive of a large bank once told a colleague of mine: 'By the time I get the key financial data out of our bank's systems, it's all but useless.'

Of course, causality still matters. But thanks to the flood of digital information and Moore's Law (which makes it cheap to capture and store data), our samples are now getting close to catching nearly every data point. And it's now that correlations become much more significant because we no longer have to theorise to understand, we can just let the correlations speak for themselves.

So we don't have to draw a direct causal line from A to B anymore. Instead we want to understand whether A (a person, sensor or device) is part of a cluster and because most people or objects in this cluster behave in a similar way, we can assume outcome B. In other words: Are A and B correlated? We could also spot outliers, for example if A deviates from the behaviour of others in its cluster.

This adds new dimensions to our data universe, and allows us to use the information in radically different ways.

Finally, because we look for correlations in a Big Data world, not causations, we don't operate based on certainty (A must cause B), but probability (there is an 85% chance that B happens if condition A has been met).

I admit, all this is currently pretty controversial. And yes, even very, very large sample sizes may throw up correlations that are flukes rather than truly related – that's why we need to subject them to critical analysis. But as we keep adding to the breadth and depth of data available, much of the discussion will become more or less moot. It's not going to happen overnight. In fact it's going to take many years, not just for the data to become available on the scale we'll require, but equally for us, the humans, to be able to adapt to the potential and new principles it offers.

THIS IS NOT A BIG DATA BOOK

Thankfully, this is not a Big Data book. But in many ways it could be because our two stories end in the same way – in a Big Data world, having more information is where success comes from. And hopefully by now you've understood that our story is going to end in just the same way. The digital deluge offers organisations and individuals huge potential, and it's not really so much about having lots of data but about using it in a completely different way.

What does this mean for today's organisations and the individuals within them? Well, the more data we create (at work and at play), the cleverer we have to be about channelling the deluge. We have to upgrade ourselves and become connected customers and connected workers. What are the tools, though, that will help consumers engage and make employees more productive? And how can all this connectivity revolutionise today's business models?

Let's look at it first from the perspective of the business: companies and their analysts don't have to be perfectionists anymore. Given they are able to capture more data than ever before, the huge size of their samples means they no longer need to be perfect. Instead, they use systems that have an inbuilt tolerance for imperfect data sets. The outcome: businesses can process information faster, do rapid trial-and-error research, draw quick conclusions, gain new insights and generally execute smarter.

Achieving this is not a question of throwing hardware at the problem; rather, the solution lies in finding a cleverer way of handling data. At Harvard University, Professor Gary King tells the story of a colleague who fretted that he needed a $2m computer to work his way through a mountain of data. Within two hours, King and his graduate students developed an algorithm that could do the work in 20 minutes – on a laptop.[35]

That's not without challenges, of course, because Big Data analytics often have to cope with an unprecedented volume, velocity and variety of data – a torrent of real-time facts and figures collected from a wide range of sources: a company's CRM system, social media analytics, accounts, sales, web server logs, PowerPoint presentations, images, videos, email and dozens of other data pools.

We don't even have to concern ourselves here with the challenge that, according to IDC, about 90% of all this data will be unstructured. Unstructured data follows no pattern other than its own and as a result falls outside of our traditional, ordered approach to data analysis.[36] But this problem is

---

35   Shaw, Jonathan (March–April 2014), "Why 'Big Data' Is a Big Deal", *Harvard Magazine* (Cambridge, Massachusetts). **harvardmagazine.com/2014/03/why-big-data-is-a-big-deal**

36   Quoted in HP (December 2012), "Information Optimization: Harness the power of Big Data", HP Business Whitepaper. **www.hp.com/hpinfo/newsroom/press_kits/2012/ HPDiscoverFrankfurt2012/IO_Whitepaper_Harness_the_Power_of_Big_Data.pdf**

quickly becoming a thing of the past. The power of data is being leveraged by the power of machines (more on this in the next chapter) through algorithms that can learn to make sense of the chaos and enable anyone to interact with it and extract information. Finally, Big Data becomes less about the technology and more about the information that lies latent within it. Just as we discovered earlier, in chapter 3, the trick is all about how we identify the useful from the useless and harness the power of the digital deluge.

And this is where much of the cultural challenge of Big Data rests, because most organisations are only just beginning to understand the hidden potential of the power of the data they already hold in their hands.

UNEARTHING BIG DATA'S TOP THREE HIDDEN TALENTS

The most common mistake we make is that, fuelled by an unreasonable fear of the digital deluge, most Big Data conversations quickly narrow down to talk about business insight and business intelligence; as a result the conversation focuses on using data to help with *existing* processes rather than discovering new opportunities. Removing the blinkers about the data you hold and looking for new ways the data could be used is the first of the three untapped opportunities Big Data offers organisations.[37]

---

37   I'm drawing for this part heavily on the most excellent book by Kenneth Cukier and Viktor Mayer-Schönberger – *Big Data: A Revolution That Will Transform How We Live, Work, and Think* (Houghton Mifflin, New York, 2013) – which I recommend to anybody interested in the power of Big Data.

All too often we don't realise that most data sets can be used for more than a single purpose. Let's take the location information that pinpoints mobile phones and helps telecoms companies to manage their networks. If all the mobile phones on a road slow down to a crawl, we can use the data to identify a traffic jam or a bottleneck in our transport system. Location data in a city allows us to estimate the size of a demonstration, or help a company decide where to open a new restaurant. Mistyped search terms help to educate spell-checking software.

Big Data gets really interesting when we look at the second new opportunity, where we link seemingly unrelated data sets and discover correlations that provide deep insight. Unusual data-mining can help credit card companies to evaluate the risk of default: people who buy anti-scuff pads for their furniture, for example, are highly likely to make their payments.[38] Logistics companies can link databases of accident black spots with route-planning software to reduce the number of accidents and wasted time. Comparing hospital readmissions across all patient categories with the information on patient accommodation can pinpoint rooms that are not cleaned properly and may result in fresh infections.

Finally, the third of Big Data's hidden talents is when data is set up to serve more than one purpose – from the CCTV system that not only catches shoplifters but also counts a store's footfall, to an online game website that not only remembers a player's progress in the game for the next session, but also identifies where the game gets too demanding, or whether the player is close to making an in-app purchase: and therefore offers him or her a discount to get them across the threshold.

---

38   (Shaw, 2014)

Much of this data collection is on purpose, some of it by accident. And a lot of valuable information goes completely unrecorded. Still, enterprise IT has resulted in an accumulation of data that for the first time has given businesses more social science data than academics hold.[39]

Slowly, companies are beginning to understand that one of their most valuable assets could be the dark or dusty data sitting largely unused in their corporate databanks. So now they are beginning to find ways of putting their internal digital deluge to work by making data insights as ubiquitous and real-time as Excel and email and in so doing seeking to establish a "data dividend" – a distribution of the informational "profits" that can be gained and shared around the organisation.

MOVING OUT OF CREEPY VALLEY

Hopefully by now you should be beginning to share my sense of potential of a Big Data world. But equally I hope that at this point of the argument, most of you will have at least two alarm bells ringing. Are computers taking over the world? And what about our privacy?

Pablo Picasso provided us with a brief answer to the first question (and I will provide a longer one in the final chapter) when he said 'Computers are useless. They can only give you answers'. Picasso was responding to a different phase of our machine age and was actually referring to "mechanical brains" and "calculating machines" in Paris in 1964, but these machines are the ancestors of our computers today, and his basic point still stands. We can amass as many data points as

---

39   *Ibid.*

we like, but to turn them into information – into something we can analyse – we have to apply a model. And to do that, we need humans that know how to ask the right questions.

Companies expect that the amount of data they have to manage will grow by 76% during the coming year or so, reports IDG Enterprise.[40] Machines will help us to sift through the digital deluge. But, once again, only humans will be able to analyse this information and turn probability into certainty.

And what about privacy? The Germans have a neat expression for our datafied world: they call the online versions of us *der gläserne Mensch* – humans that to the observer are as transparent as glass.

Some companies have started to equip workers with sensors that help monitor movements and interaction. In a trial, Bank of America spotted that a team's productivity could be boosted by scheduling coffee breaks for the whole team, because it resulted in better collaboration. A technology company discovered that teams became more productive when the tables in the canteen were large enough for 12 people rather than four, because it resulted in more social interaction across the team, according to Dr Ben Waber, chief executive of Sociometric Solutions.

But as the *Wall Street Journal* notes, such data collection treads 'a fine line between Big Data and Big Brother.'[41]

---

40   IDG Enterprise (6 January 2014), "Big Data: Growing Trends and Emerging Opportunities", Research Report. **www.idgenterprise.com/report/big-data-2**

41   Silverman, Rachel Emma (7 March 2013), "Tracking Sensors Invade the Workplace", *Wall Street Journal* (New York). **online.wsj.com/news/articles/SB10001424127887324034804578344303429080678**

Then there's biomedical data, where privacy problems multiply. 'As soon as you touch genomic data, that information is fundamentally identifiable,' says John Quackenbush, a professor of computational biology and bioinformatics. 'I can erase your address and Social Security number and every other identifier, but I can't anonymize your genome without wiping out the information that I need to analyze.'[42]

Even without advances in new types of data becoming available, we face major challenges in maintaining the privacy of the individuals whose data we hold. A Big Data world places a massive strain on all of our existing privacy infrastructure (both legal, regulatory and cultural) and we should not expect it to cope. Left as it is, this framework will fail.

We must recognise that many of the huge opportunities of Big Data and the seductive nature of that hidden value I described earlier will entice individuals and organisations into areas that will cause problems – unless we step up now and establish new rules and principles that protect both individuals and organisations, and enable us to extract the value without doing harm. Whether it is as simple as adapting privacy policies for data re-use (a potential minefield if trust and value have yet to be established) or more innovative approaches like "vendor relationship management" (VRM) solutions that give individuals more control about their own data. VRM sounds complex, but it is simply an inversion of the current data model, where instead of the organisation holding all my data, I hold it myself and allow the organisation access through a trusted third party.

---

42   (Shaw, 2014)

I know I'm repeating myself, but we are the first generation of Big Data users. We have to decide how much data usage we are comfortable with. Sometimes it's a question of getting used to something. As Kenneth Cukier and Viktor Mayer-Schönberger note in their seminal book, *Big Data*, the biggest data collector of them all, Facebook, 'has been shrewdly patient, knowing that unveiling too many new purposes for its users' data too soon could freak them out'.

Once again, it all comes down to transparency: companies, organisations and governments have to be open about what they do with our data, and they have to be clear what we get in return – or how we can opt out of the system (and the cost of doing that).

CREATING A DATA CULTURE

As we begin to understand the power (and the potential pitfalls) of data, we need to look for the skills and resources that individuals and organisations are going to need to work with and get the most from the digital deluge.

Much has been said about how important it is for organisations to find the right people that can help them navigate through this new world of data. Many people (including myself) joke that the next generation of data scientists will be the new rock-stars of the corporate world.

But it's wrong to put all the focus on the numbers. After all, we've already established that Big Data is not about handling the data but interpreting it properly instead.

It's this skill that the data scientists need to achieve rock-star status.

The science of Big Data requires a multi-disciplinary approach. The basic skills are, of course, mathematics, statistics and computer science, but they alone are not enough. Data science should be part machine, part human, and as a result the goal should be to blend creative skills that augment and extend technical capabilities.

In particular, skills like anthropology, entrepreneurism and yes, even storytelling (I'm serious) are all essential. If you can't be creative about what the data might be able to tell you, you'll never be innovative about what you might do with it. People will need to not just make sense of the data but see the value in relation to the real world.

Once again, the culture of the organisation is crucial here. Organisations are going to need to foster a data-friendly environment where the power of data and of the digital deluge is celebrated, and individuals are empowered and encouraged to explore in order to find ways to improve the outcomes for their firm.

As a result, the future Big Data economy is going to require new skills, tools and ideas that do it justice and help organisations channel and harness the power of the digital deluge. But in order to achieve this, we need to understand that our biggest challenge and opportunity lies, as always, in our relationship with the machines – it is they that control the flow of information. Understanding the potential of the machines and how we can best work with them is the ultimate answer to harnessing the digital deluge. And that is what we will explore next.

Small data and a bright future, by Lutz Finger

Data everywhere

DATA IS NOTHING new. We have been creating data for centuries. For example, the Incas measured time using two pillars of stone in the 15th century, to know when to plant their crops.

What has changed since then? The amount of data we produce. Everything from a simple email to the onboard computers in our cars leaves a broad trail of data nowadays. We are living in a mind-blowing world of big data: exabytes of daily information trending ever upwards.

Big data changes our world

We hear lots of inspiring stories about the value in this data. The police will be able to predict crime before it happens. Health checks will predict illnesses before they reach us.

Big data is indeed creating new opportunities that are changing whole ecosystems. Take the media industry as an example. The demand for media has not changed. More media then ever is consumed. New business models are appearing that did not exist before. Recommendation services such as Amazon or Netflix are only made possible through data.

We want small data

More data alone does not mean more business models or more insights. We all know this from personal experience. Since we digitalized our personal photos we now have 10× or 100× more of them. However, these photos need to be stored, tagged, and sorted...which is actually more work than the old times where we had only a few real prints.

Your personal issues with too many photos are true for business as well. More data means more pain. It means more issues in handling the data and finding what you really want. Let's look back at the Incas. They wanted to know only one thing: when to plant the crops. This is not big data. This is a binary decision. Yes or no. This has not changed. You as a leader need to make binary decisions as well. Should I buy this company or not? Should we run this marketing campaign or not? Should we hire someone or not? What you want is small data, not big data.

Should we then dismiss all those big data discussions? No, not at all. Some things only work because we have big data. LinkedIn can only recommend a company with certain values or certain types of jobs to a person because we have big data. Many of the services we offer today with 277 million members would not have been possible with just 10 million. This long tail of data is important.

However, the important part is to reduce this data so you are looking at the right metric. I have seen many companies mistake data-driven decisions for an obsession with numbers. They take all the possible metrics they can measure, cram it into a dashboard, and ask their management to review it daily. More is not better here: most businesses have only a few focus points, and keeping it simple is a good rule for dealing with data.

Ask – measure – learn

How do we get to a simple way of steering your business through massive amounts of data? It is a three-step approach:

- ask the right question.

- use the right data and

- learn and take actions upon it.

Take AltaVista, the search engine. It measured many things about URLs. It was proud to classify much of the web. But it was the simple metric of Google's PageRank that halved its business in just 12 months. Before you start collecting and measuring data – for example, all of your customers' social media discussions – **ask** yourself why, what you will **measure**, and what you can **learn** from it.

If you follow these rules, the future of data is promising. Here are some examples:

- Benchmarking performance – for example, which marketing campaign performed better?

- Recommendations – such as who you might know on LinkedIn.

- Prediction – Target, for example, uses its loyalty card data to predict whether someone is pregnant and market directly to them.

If you use data effectively for any of these three areas you might find new, or change existing, business models. And if you do so, your future will be bright. Because one thing has not changed since the time of the Incas: the one who knows how to create value – whether it is when to plant maize or how to target customers – becomes the ruler.

Go and build the future out of data.

Lutz Finger, a director at LinkedIn, is an authority on social media and text analytics.

'By the time Skynet became self-aware it had spread into millions of computer servers across the planet. Ordinary computers in office buildings, dorm rooms; everywhere. It was software; in cyberspace. There was no system core; it could not be shutdown. The attack began at 6:18 PM, just as he said it would. Judgment Day, the day the human race was almost destroyed by the weapons they'd built to protect themselves.'

– JOHN CONNOR, LEADER OF THE WORLDWIDE HUMAN RESISTANCE

HOW I LEARNED TO STOP WORRYING AND LOVE THE ALGORITHMS

FOR A COUPLE OF hundred years the advent of technology has been a disruptive force in our society, driving change and causing hardship for those unable to keep up. In many ways, today's world is no different.

Technology continues to evolve at an increasing rate and we humans often struggle beneath the digital deluge. But I'm not trying to frighten anyone, or even fan the flames of dissent about the role of technology. In reality I think the problems of our future are nowhere near as bleak as often suggested. The robot apocalypse is not actually imminent.

But I do worry about the future, and sometimes I am frightened – just not by the machines. I worry instead that we as the first generation of Big Data users might blow it and fail to learn how to handle all this information, that we will allow ourselves to be buried by the digital deluge rather than learn how to thrive on it.

This is the task that lies in front of us. We need to master the skills that allow us to use the power of the machines and harness the digital deluge and in so doing, adjust our culture (and laws) to accommodate their potential in a safe, productive way; we have to channel the flow of information and add Big Data analytics to our tool set. And that's true not just for companies and their staff, but for customers and consumers too.

But first, we have to understand the direction in which we, the humans, are sending machines. Thankfully, real life is not *The Terminator* and the internet is not Skynet. Instead, it's us technologists not the cyborg brains of the future who are pushing the boundaries and have to understand both the potential and the limitations of what machines can achieve.

Unsurprisingly, that means the biggest barrier to the rise of the machines is ourselves. And it's not actually a good thing.

THE END OF HANDMADE DIGITAL

Until recently, most solutions to channel the digital deluge – from email programs and social media feeds to enterprise resource planning software and business intelligence suites – have been crafted by hand. Legions of programmers have coded each line of software to enable processes and workflows designed by a software developer.

The results can be powerful, but it's a process that has two flaws: it's standardised and it's static. In other words, chances are the software does not quite meet my needs, or it does so only some of the time, for certain uses. More importantly, if my needs change – because my interests shift or I work differently – I have to recalibrate all the software settings and data feeds by hand.

This is the dominant model for producing digital tools, but it's steeped in the past and not future-proof. It reflects a less-connected world, a small data era when the internet was used by only a tiny subset of our society and the transformative power of the cloud was yet to be realised.

As data sources and volumes explode, through the digital deluge we are gaining exponentially better access to even more information. And that's even before the Internet of Things delivers its payload of a seemingly infinite world of connected devices and entities pouring out real-time status updates: the basis of an incredibly rich and powerful mesh of data.

Already, most cars have vastly more computing power than the first Space Shuttle. Our phones are starting to capture our health metrics. At home we are beginning to connect refrigerators, air conditioning and heating, and even light bulbs to the internet; at work, companies weave a web of connectivity around both staff and customers, gaining deeper insight, providing better services and boosting productivity. A few years ago it was forecast that by 2020 around 50 billion "things" and devices would be connected to the internet. The most recent forecast, by IDC, puts that number at a staggering 212 billion.[43]

To tie all this together, to make it work, we can no longer code solutions by hand. We can't rely on traditional managerial decision-making. Humanity neither has the capacity nor the agility to keep up with the speed at which our world is developing.

Once again the solution has one common denominator – data.

TEACHING THE MACHINES TO LEARN

Nearly 60 years ago, a new form of computer science was established, one that instead of being driven by instructions fed by a programmer, relied on the statistical analysis of data. Although perhaps not realised at the time, it is in fact likely one of the most pivotal moments of our technological evolution.

It was the beginning of machine learning.

This is another one of those wonderful computer science phrases that does its best to put the fear of God into most people, but it is essentially the future of our relationship with technology. It is the most feasible means by which vast swathes

---

43   IDC (3 October 2013), "The Internet of Things Is Poised to Change Everything, Says IDC", IDC press release. **www.idc.com/getdoc.jsp?containerId=prUS24366813**

of data can be analysed, patterns recognised and meaning inferred without falling foul of inflexibility or incapacity.

Unlike traditional computer programming, machine-learning algorithms don't follow a strict set of unbreakable instructions. Instead, they work against a model, crafted by humans, that sets the framework that guides their usage and interpretation of data – which is then used to teach themselves the rules as to how a specific context operates.

It's probably best explained using a few examples. Machine learning is already providing a new generation of transformative services that we are increasingly relying on to help us navigate through the digital deluge in our everyday lives.

The first example I'll give is language translation. Do you remember the software-based language translators of old? Well, I do, and I remember how hilarious they were to work with, because the way in which they were built simply couldn't cope with the ambiguous nature of language. Back then, it was a world of dictionaries and rules. Typing the word "cat" would result in a dictionary-based look-up and the response of, say, "chat", for the French translation. Typing something more complex – "Je suis un rock-star", for example – would likely result in something even more hilarious than Bill Wyman's original lyrics.

The thing is, our language doesn't follow rules. In actual fact, they're more like guidelines really. At school, we are taught them as if they are as inflexible and strict as the laws of physics and we forget that, unlike gravity and Newton's laws of motion, with language, rules can be bent and changed.

The "i" before "e" rule is a classic example of this. When we're kids, we're taught "i before e except after c" but the reality is that there are actually more exceptions to the rule than the rule itself. (There are in fact 923 exceptions in the English language.) Not much of a rule, is it?

So in a world of flawed and flexible rules, how on earth can we expect traditional approaches to work? Thankfully, language translation has recently switched to a machine-learning approach, one that uses a statistical model based on *patterns of words* rather than a 1:1 connection and this provides enough latitude to cope with much more of the ambiguity and nuance that complex language can throw at it. Using this and some of the recent developments in machine learning around deep neural networks (essentially a breakthrough that uses layers of pattern recognition – a method inspired by the way neurons function in the brain) it now means we can, from a relatively small body of data, create a service that can accurately translate between languages. This service is becoming so powerful (Microsoft demonstrated it being used for live, real-time speech back in December 2012)[44] that it starts to present incredible new opportunities for our society. For example, should I bother to get my eight-year-old son to learn a foreign language? (The answer is, of course, yes, but perhaps more for cultural than academic reasons.)

The second example is how statistical-based machine learning can massively simplify the creation of complex systems that enable transformative new experiences like the Xbox Kinect

---

44   Rashid, Rick (8 November 2012), "Microsoft Research shows a promising new breakthrough in speech translation technology", *Next At Microsoft*. **blogs.technet.com/b/ next/archive/2012/11/08/microsoft-research-shows-a-promising-new-breakthrough- in-speech-translation-technology.aspx#.Uz6VVu9OXcs**

and other natural forms of computer interaction. The Kinect observes the movements of the human player in front of the television, and reflects them in real-time through an avatar on the screen. It would have been impossible to handcraft an algorithm that takes account of the myriad movements a human might make. Instead, the team gave the machine a model of the human body, and through constant learning the machine was able to develop an algorithm that can predict the probable location for every body part – and translate that into the avatar on the screen.

Such machines – or rather their algorithms – 'self-tune to accumulated knowledge and changing circumstances'.[45]

In other words:

1. Machine-learning systems make predictions (e.g. "this must be spam", "the leg moves look like this") based on experiences drawn from a huge trove of "training" data.

2. Machines can only learn from data by processing it within a model that has been given to them; they can't learn from data alone.

3. As the volume of data expands, the machines learn from the results of previous predictions and fine-tune the model. This iterative self-improvement is one of the most powerful features of machine learning and yet it remains a key limitation as the learning is still confined within the constraints of the original model.

---

45   Reeves, Martin; Nicol, Ron; Venema, Thijs; Wittenburg, George (February 2014), "The Evolvable Enterprise: Lessons from the New Technology Giants", Boston Consulting Group. **www.bcg.com/expertise_impact/publications/PublicationDetails. aspx?id=tcm:12-154402**

4. The machines draw conclusions and develop solutions based on probability; they are not sentient.

That doesn't mean, though, that they're not getting pretty clever. Having realised that the old deterministic model for programming (based on the certainty of an outcome that could be expressed either as 0 or 1) doesn't quite hack it in a machine-learning world, developers now create models that turn computers into probabilistic inference machines – systems that are OK with a fair bit of uncertainty.

By giving the machines an open model based on a few parameters, you can have a digital assistant like Cortana (or, if you prefer, Now, or Siri) that infers and more importantly, learns, from your data points – your diary, your emails, your web searches, your GPS data, your social media interactions – and knows that you are on the move; that you are meeting three friends; that you have a diary clash; that the train you planned to take is delayed and that there's an alternative route that will get you there faster; that alerts your friends that you're running a few minutes late; that knows you like a certain coffee chain and makes recommendations for a branch near your meeting point; and that is aware that you were planning on watching a movie later on and suggests a cinema nearby showing one made by your favourite director.

Ultra-helpful? Or ultra-creepy? That's the beauty of using a model: you yourself can set the parameters for how much support you find helpful, and what lines the machine shouldn't cross.

It will take time for us to get comfortable with this kind of machine-driven insight. Undoubtedly, many of us will have trouble adjusting to all this helpfulness (just watch whenever Facebook rolls out an update; the outcry is huge, until it's a must-have feature) and it will be down to the service providers to be transparent enough and to give us enough control to help us adapt.

The same holds true in business: just think how customer service will be transformed once a business truly understands and anticipates the needs and wants and worries of a customer from the very first point of contact. Picture how a machine-learning system working within a company can leverage the four dimensions of the connected customer that we described in chapter 4 to connect just the right people, pull together just the right knowledge, spot the problems and avoid inefficiencies at just the right time.

Once again, the key will be transparency: companies must communicate clearly what they are doing, why they are doing it, and what the costs and benefits are – at every level. And, blindingly obviously, it has to actually work.

THE SINGULARITY IS NEAR (ISH)

So far, so futuristic, but let's address the biggest concern of all: will machines one day get so clever that they'll replace us? The singularity (the moment in time when the machines become smarter than humans) is predicted to be frighteningly close by some. (Roughly 2040 if you average out a broad range of predictions.)

Well, the machines *will* get cleverer and in some cases you might even call them cleverer than us, but the singularity will likely not play out in the dystopian sci-fi way some expect. Instead, it will be a good thing, a development that lifts human beings to be able to achieve more.

And in reality machines have been doing just that for centuries now. Otherwise we'd still be sitting in front of our weaving looms or jumping on a horse instead of getting into a car. There'd still be the old kind of "computers" – the word used to just mean humans who were experts in making laborious calculations – instead of computers of the silicon variety.

As with all big shifts since the beginning of the Industrial Revolution, it's going to be a bumpy ride. As one critic wrote: 'The dirty secret of the digital economy is that humans do not know how to fight back'.[46]

But we do. We just have to understand that the digital deluge is a huge opportunity for us and that Big Data and machine learning are simply the new tools we're going to need to make the best of that opportunity. And like any new tool, as it replaces work we used to do, we shift our area of expertise to the next level.

Eric Schmidt (Google's executive chairman) warned recently that 'the race is between computers and people and the people need to win…In this fight, it is very important that we find the things that humans are really good at.'[47]

---

46   Tett, Gillian (28 March 2014), "Digital v human: the new debate", *Financial Times*. **www.ft.com/cms/s/2/74875576-b539-11e3-af92-00144feabdc0.html**

47   Gapper, John and Waters, Richard (23 January 2014), "Google chief warns of IT threat", *Financial Times*. **www.ft.com/cms/s/0/206bb2e2-847f-11e3-b72e-00144feab7de.html**

First we need to look at what machines and algorithms are good at. They are great for doing boring automated tasks, crunching numbers and sifting through huge amounts of data. They can replace 'any mental activity that involves following a set of rules'.[48] They can keep things ticking over. They are good at spotting the "normal", the cluster, but don't know what to do with the exception. They can help us navigate through the digital deluge but they are not able to use intuition, improvise or be creative. That's because by their very model-based nature they understand only correlation, not causation.

And that's where we humans excel: we can make sense of it all. Without our models, the data we feed the machines is just noise. Unless we write them a script they have no clue how to deal with a crisis. And what happens when events go completely off the map and do something improbable? A machine may be able to predict a disaster, but it almost certainly won't know how to cope with it or react as the complexity of any such event plays out.

And there are other limitations that will continue to push the singularity horizon further and further back. In the 1980s, Hans Moravec and a few of his colleagues established "Moravec's paradox" – essentially the fact that contrary to our traditional assumptions, high-level reasoning requires comparatively little computation, but low-level sensor motor skills require enormous computational resources.

Put simply, you can teach a machine the rules of Kerplunk, but getting it to pick up and move the pieces is almost impossible.

---

48   Brooks, David (3 February 2014), "What Machines Can't Do", *New York Times*.
www.nytimes.com/2014/02/04/opinion/brooks-what-machines-cant-do.html

It's a bit like IBM's Watson, or Deep Blue, both artificially intelligent super computers that famously could beat the best of the best of humans in a game of Jeopardy or chess. But even they can only operate within the models they have been provided with. Despite all their horsepower and computational speed I could still beat both of them with one arm tied behind my back at a game of Go Fish or noughts-and-crosses.

So while a good algorithm can "write" a business report, or even a data-driven news story – whether it's breaking news about an earthquake or a factual report about a football match – the machine won't understand the strategy or the troubles of a company, capture the terror and the humanity of a disaster, or convey the passion and excitement of a game.

As the chess master Gary Kasparov once observed, after playing on a team with a chess computer, the machine possessed more 'tactical acuity', while he possessed greater 'strategic guidance'.[49]

These challenges combine to underline the crucial role that humans will continue to need to play and why our future lies entirely in the reality of humans *plus* machines rather than *versus* them.

'Machines now handle a lot of tasks for us, so humans need to concentrate on building the skills that machines can't do – jobs will change as a result as we need to reimagine how we work with computers.'[50]

---

49 *Ibid.*

50 Brynjolfsson, Erik and McAffe, Andrew (2014), *The Second Machine Age: Work, Progress, and Prosperity in a Time of Brilliant Technologies* (W. W. Norton & Company, Inc., New York).

WHAT SEEMS HARD IS EASY, WHAT SEEMS EASY IS HARD

The biggest impact of the new world of machine learning will likely be felt by today's knowledge workers as these will be the roles most likely replaced by machines. Moravec's paradox tells us that other more manual roles traditionally deemed to be less valuable (at least in terms of financial compensation) will be secure for decades to come.

But before the knowledge workers form their own Luddite rebellion (how ironic would that be?) we've just got to remember that by getting the machines to do more work, more of the heavy lifting, we should be pushing ourselves to make better use of that platform to extend ourselves further.

It's no different to the debate we had when I was a kid at school, at a time when pocket calculators were first becoming affordable and produced for the mass market. I did the majority of my mathematics exams armed with no more than a slide rule and a log book (and I did OK thanks very much) but let me tell you, I am a better mathematician with a calculator than I am with a book of tabulated paper and slidy bit of plastic. Yes, I need to know the basic principles of arithmetic but I can get the machine to take care of the heavy lifting. We no longer have that debate and our culture and curriculums have adapted to integrate the power of the calculator to lift human beings to be able to do more and more complex calculations. Our relationship with algorithms and machine learning should be no different.

Learning how to write computer code is certainly useful, but it's not a must. What will be a vital skill, however, is the ability to understand and analyse data, and to know the limits of what machines can do. If we fail to do that, we'll end up like the driver who blindly follows the suggestions of the satellite navigation software and ends up stuck in a narrow road or marooned at a river crossing.

Like pocket calculators, machine learning and algorithms will become more and more accessible to everyone, increasingly moving out of the huge computational power of cloud-based data centres and into our hands and the devices on our desks. Just as the personal computer revolution brought us an increasingly powerful and yet accessible array of functionality, so too will the machine-learning revolution bring us the incredible transformative power of algorithms at the click of a button or in response to a natural (i.e. human) command.

Machine learning will be the thing that most powerfully turns the "constraint" of the digital deluge into the liberating force it should be. It will make connections for us that we never knew about; it might even answer questions that we probably didn't realise we needed to ask. For routine tasks, the machines will even make decisions on our behalf. However, it will take humans to make sense of it all – to create, to generate ideas and innovate.

Our only challenge is to regain control, to make conscious choices about where technology is best placed to help, and just as importantly, where it is not. Finally, it is time for us to break free of the chains we have created for ourselves by sleepwalking into technological developments and allowing ourselves to drown in the digital deluge.

Technology offers our society so much. But it is up to us, the humans, to rise to that potential.

'I do not fear computers. I fear the lack of them.'

– ISAAC ASIMOV

JUDGEMENT DAY

SO I'VE PICKED enough holes in everyone else's vision of the future – it's time I shared my own.

The digital deluge will continue. The temptation of making technology do things *for* us rather than *with* us (with human and technological potential both losing out) will remain. The world's population will become more connected and the Internet of Things will reach parts of our physical world that we can't even imagine. Connectivity will be constant and universal.

And I'm an optimist. I don't think we'll allow technology to overwhelm us.

Instead, we will harness connectivity and use Big Data models to power an 'era of assistants', where 'algorithms embodied as robots or avatars provide solutions to problems, facilitate decision-making, measure performance and in general, take care of most routine tasks'.[51]

My vision of the future is not HAL 9000. Instead it is much more *Halo*'s Cortana (and a precursor of that fully-fledged sci-fi AI already lives in my phone), where transparent "automated judgements" harness the power and potential of the digital deluge which then complement, not replace, our ability to think deep.

None of us know exactly how this future will play out. As Gillian Tett writes in the *Financial Times*: 'we have barely begun to understand the full implications of this second, digitised economy'.[52]

---

51   Corsello, Jason (19 November 2013), "What the Internet of Things Will Bring to the Workplace", *Wired* blog. **www.wired.com/insights/2013/11/what-the-internet-of-things-will-bring-to-the-workplace**

52   (Tett, 2014)

Of course, we have to remain mindful of the digital bear traps: as we rely more and more on smartphones and their "map-reading skills", we must not lose our spatial awareness. We don't need to remember all phone numbers and facts, it's OK to tuck knowledge away in the silicon folds of our smartphone and cloud computing world, but we must train our memories to focus on connecting the dots. We need to be conscious of our quest for "more" when sometimes we should focus on "better", ensuring that throughout we strike the right balance between consumption and creation.

There are tasks and capabilities that we can happily outsource to the machines, and there are some where we will want to double-task, and there will be many that we'll have to learn for the first time. We need to be aware of our instinctive preference for "low-hanging fruit" and instead remember that sometimes we need to take the time to exert a little more effort for the sweeter, more nourishing bounty that may be found just beyond our initial reach.

For us humans, it all comes down to having the right skillset, as we apply the most powerful, the most complex computers in this world – our brains – to new tasks.

The machines, in turn, also have some learning to do. They have to get better at understanding human context and human emotion.[53] And so, one day, we may partner with machines that have human-like qualities. But the algorithms won't be on a par with humans.

---

53   Taylor, Paul (20 August 2013), "Lines blurring between humans and machines", *Financial Times*. **www.ft.com/cms/s/0/b69e879a-09c2-11e3-ad07-00144feabdc0.html**

Every year, a small group of humans and a small group of "bots" come together to take the "Turing test". The goal is simple: convince a group of judges that you are human. It's a blind test (the candidates are all unseen) that takes the form of a written conversation, and while the bots have made spectacular progress in coming across as human, so far they have failed to make the grade. It's always been humans who have come across as the "most human human", as described in Brian Christian's book of the same name, an often amusing account about his experiences participating in the Turing test, and his exploration of what it means to be human.[54]

This quest to be the most human human demonstrates that computers can get very clever. One day they may even pass the Turing test. But even if they will be able to affect a passable or uncannily human resemblance, all they'll do is provide a pastiche of human interaction – driven and informed by Big Data, probability and correlation. They will not be sentient themselves.

It's only humans that can provide the all-important architecture and models that will shape the machines' work.[55]

There's been a lot of talk about artificial intelligence. But AI is extremely limited; capable of mastering a few highly specific fields of expertise, like interpreting search queries, playing chess or providing language translation services. These AIs 'operate within an extremely specific frame of

---

54   Christian, Brian (2011), *The Most Human Human: What Artificial Intelligence Teaches Us About Being Alive* (Doubleday, New York).

55   (Brooks, 2014)

reference. They don't make conversation at parties. They're intelligent, but only if you define intelligence in a vanishingly narrow way.'[56]

That's why it's not machines, but humans, that will be truly rising in the years ahead.

NEW SKILLS FOR A NEW MACHINE AGE

Still, this transition to what Erik Brynjolfsson and Andrew McAfee have called 'The Second Machine Age' (in their great book of the same title) will not come about without massive disruptions.

As both note, 'there's never been a better time to be a worker with special skills or the right education, because these people can use technology to create and capture value. However, there's never been a worse time to be a worker with only "ordinary" skills and abilities to offer, because computers, robots, and other digital technologies are acquiring these skills and abilities at an extraordinary rate.'[57]

These are not just job skills, but life skills too. How do we learn to love not fear the digital deluge? How do we connect, how do we sort the flow of information from our social networks? When do we snack, and how can we relearn to go deep again? How can we create the right conditions for serendipity? To take time to search for true meaning as well as simple analysis

56 Grossman, Lev (10 February 2011), "2045: The Year Man Becomes Immortal", *Time Magazine.* **moodle2.portage.k12.wi.us/pluginfile.php/12287/mod_resource/content/1/ Singularity_Kurzweil_on_2045_When_Humans_Machines_Merge_--_Printout_--_TIME. pdf**

57 (Brynjolfsson and McAfee, 2014)

and in so doing ensure we design frameworks that connect the digital dots and knowledge and correlations on purpose?

That's only possible if we make the right choices: it's OK to snack on information – say when I watch a movie and browse Facebook at the same time – as long as I accept that I'm not giving either my full attention. Sleepwalking into that choice as many currently do is not going to enhance anyone's experience and the value of what could have been transformative will be lost.

Snacking, however, can't be our survival mechanism to cope with the data flood – above all because it's just not a very good one. The same goes for bingeing. We have to change our personal culture, and we have to change our corporate culture, and we have to develop the right tools. We have to learn to use technology so that it puts us in control.

We have to learn not just to survive but to *thrive*.

Along the way, we have to define our comfort level on issues like privacy. There will be plenty of crunch points. What's the right trade-off between the value of our own personal data and the (free) services we may receive? Are we happy to be "transparent", and what's the cost of being off-the-grid?

The same holds true inside our organisations: how much should a company give away of its inner workings in return for the benefit of frictionless interaction with customers and enterprise partners or how far should they break down semi-dysfunctional internal silos in order to become more responsive and agile?

Our current organisational failures are not so much the result of stupid (or power-hungry) managers, but are instead because of a natural desire to have business units that are a manageable and human size. The drawback inherent in this approach is that it traps expertise and knowledge and data. That's not just inefficient, it can also end in corporate disaster. Just think of Lehman Brothers: one of the reasons for the investment bank's collapse was that information about risk exposure was fragmented and therefore poorly understood.

We can guard against such risk – and spot opportunities – by using new tools to join up the disparate data streams and parsing them with clever algorithms that break down corporate barriers and allow us the potential of true serendipity. But we must not stop there. The next step will be to use technology to ensure we have tools that provide us with intelligent and deliberate discovery.

So when I talk about how connectivity and Big Data will change the enterprise, I'm not talking about better business intelligence. It's about how technology will help us harness and exploit the digital deluge, and in so doing bring about a complete transformation of business.

We have to 'foster an exploratory mindset...strengthen dynamic information management... [and] build an experimentation engine', in a system that 'continually tune[s] your algorithm', as a study by Boston Consulting Group recommends.[58]

And when it comes to customers, it's up to each company to reassure them that it's got their best interests in mind, rather than just its own.

---

58   (Reeves et al., 2014)

THE RISING TIDE

The genesis of this book was actually a couple of years ago. It was a quiet Saturday morning in the Coplin household. With my wife busy upstairs, I was on duty, tasked with both looking after my son (then six years old) and cooking lunch. Thankfully, these are both tasks that I enjoy and am able to complete with some degree of success. My challenge, however, was that I could not complete both simultaneously; multi-tasking as we now know is not something at which we humans excel (although at the time I simply put it down to the challenges of my gender).

I solved the problem by employing a digital baby-sitter – and left my son ensconced with his Nintendo DS while I concentrated on whatever complex culinary creation we were intending to enjoy on that particular day. Ten minutes later, my son comes bursting into the kitchen shouting 'Dad, Dad, Dad! You've got to help me, I'm stuck on *Mario and Luigi: Partners in Time*, World 5, Bowser Level! You've just got to help!' And I'm looking at the food burning on the stove, and looking at him, and I realise I face an almost impossible dilemma.

I call upon the full extent of my skills of fatherhood and tell him, with some confidence, that I will be with him in 'five minutes'.

Fifteen minutes later, I've finally finished cooking when I suddenly remember that I've neglected the other part of my duties. Panicking, I seek out my son and find him in my office sat in front of a search engine. He's typed in a query: 'Mario and Luigi Partners in Time Walkthrough'.

It was a crucial moment for me as a geek dad. While my wife remembers his first steps, his first words, I ran up the stairs, tears welling in my eyes, shouting to my wife: 'You're not going to believe what he's just done – he's just formed his first search query! I'm so proud!'

Because what my son had done was, in its simple way, a perfect embryonic example of the opportunity that technology offers all of us. If you're lucky, when you're six years old, not being able to beat Bowser in World 5 in *Mario and Luigi: Partners in Time* is probably the biggest problem you've faced in your entire life. He sat there, drew on all of his knowledge and experience, and used technology to *lift* his potential, to extend beyond what he alone was capable of. He used it to augment his abilities and ultimately solve his problem.

I've spent many a time reflecting on that moment (and boring people with the story) and it really rammed home the danger that we face if we get this wrong and continue to miss the transformational potential on offer. Technology should be the rising tide that lifts all boats. It is a force that should provide a platform on which we humans can stand and extend our reach to achieve great things, be they at work or at play.

We – the first generation of connected consumers, connected workers and connected companies in a Big Data world – have big challenges to tackle and it's not going to be easy. The task ahead looks daunting. But the opportunities and rewards ahead are even greater.

At the heart of the solution will be skills; and they will have to be flexible, constantly evolving skills – not least as we don't know how technology will develop.

Remember the 1980s, when we were told that we would have to learn Japanese in order to survive in the world economy? What are today's "must-have" skill that may be superfluous in five or ten years' time? Touch typing? Writing computer code? Learning Mandarin? The answer is hard to spot, but thankfully the principle for how to adapt is easy to find.

We need to stop thinking about today's tools because they will likely not be the tools of tomorrow. Instead we need to focus on skills. Skills that will help us thrive in the digital deluge – like critical thinking, effective communication, creativity, entrepreneurship and engineering (all in their broadest sense) – will not just always be relevant but also will ensure that individuals can continue to rise up with the flowing technological tide and achieve more than was previously possible.

What's clear is that the second machine age will empower us like no technology has before. 'The best combination for problem solving is a human and a computer', says Neil Jacobstein, the head of artificial intelligence at Singularity University.[59] And he wasn't talking about a world of cyborgs and androids.

We need to remember that the machines and their algorithms are here to help. The success of our future will depend entirely on our ability to grasp the potential they offer us. As a result, our aspiration should be to do things *differently*, not the same things slightly better.

---

59   www.bbc.co.uk/news/technology-25000756

If we get this right, we humans won't have to be in awe of the machines; nor will we be drowning beneath a digital deluge. Instead, we will stand high and proud on the shoulders of these mechanical giants and accomplish truly amazing things. The time for us to make this happen is now. The rise of the humans has already started – and the world will never be the same again.

Acknowledgements

TO A GREAT EXTENT this book has very much been our difficult second album. Buoyed by the success of our first book and full of ideas, we had much to live up to. Thankfully, there was a whole host of people who were willing to rise up and join us in our battle to save ourselves from potential oppression by our digital overlords:

First and foremost I'd like to thank everyone who joined us in the conversation we started with *Business Reimagined*. It was through your enthusiasm and engagement that we knew we wanted to do more.

We were blessed to meet new friends and contact old ones who all took time out of their own schedules and initiatives to share their ideas and experiences and in so doing help shape our story. In particular I'd like to thank Guy Clapperton, Tony Crabbe, Lutz Finger, Professor Gloria Mark, Adam Pisoni and Dr Nerina Ramlakhan – they are all incredible thought leaders and we were so lucky to have them with us.

The organ grinder of this particular operation remains Nick Morris. Permanently at the heart of all of the activity, quietly orchestrating our success and tirelessly ensuring we remain connected to our audience and our stakeholders. His ability to stay calm and manage the "creative cycle" (i.e. long periods of procrastination followed by manic periods of writing) is legendary. A good friend, ready to challenge and extend beyond his day job and always focused on what he can do to make others successful. When thinking about the workforce of the future, all I really know for sure is that I hope it's filled with people like him.

When I spoke to Nick about the idea for this book, he knew we'd need some help in bringing the story to life and so he introduced us to Tim Weber, a journalist of some repute. Tim brought insight, rigour and humour to our content and helped turn a ramshackle bundle of ideas into a narrative that, quite frankly, may well save humanity as we know it.

Tom Waller, Lucy Davies, Gerry Wisniewski and the rest of the fantastic team at Edelman were instrumental in not just getting us here, but with a level of passion, polish and precision that we simply could not have achieved on our own.

As always, I am indebted to the families of this core team who have put in long hours on top of busy day jobs to help us get this far.

Outside of this core, there are several other people who deserve to be called out for their part in helping us deliver this story:

Mike Harvey, our old friend from our original outing, took the time to bring some "humanity" to a mechanical dialogue and helped us expose the golden thread that linked everything we have been saying.

David Stewart, the ultimate librarian, has curated our knowledge and nudged us in the right direction for years.

It was David that helped us find Harriman House, our publishers, and that has proved to have been one of the most wonderful connections to date. Myles Hunt, Chris Parker and Sally Tickner have all been so supportive (and patient). It's been a real pleasure to feel part of the Harriman House family; they helped us reach places we could never have reached and restored my faith in the importance and power of a good publisher in these digital times.

Microsoft continue to be brilliant in their support. Not just in providing an incredible vista (pun intended) from which it becomes easy to see the amazing opportunity technology places at our feet, but equally in the people that surround me every single day. It's intoxicating to work in a company where everyone is engaged and empowered to want to make good things happen.

Last, but by no means least, I need to thank my own family, without whose help and support I quite literally wouldn't be here.

For my mum and dad, who always provided both the inspiration and aspiration to achieve more. I'm not sure I ever tell them that enough but now I've written it down in public hopefully that might help.

For my son, John, who remains my most important reason for wanting to get the future right. But better than that, because he inspires me every single day with his own expectations and experiences with technology. I love that he embraces the opportunity that technology offers him and incorporates it so naturally into everyday life. (And no, that doesn't mean you can have some extra console time on *Minecraft*.)

And finally, waiting at the back of the queue as always, is Margaret. Margaret unwittingly takes the Turing test every single day and after 23 years is still patiently waiting to find signs of human life at the other end of the conversation. She is without doubt the "most human human" and I simply could not have achieved any of this without her support, love and understanding. It is because of the work she takes on that I am afforded the luxury of pursuing these ideas and writing them down, and I know it's going to take a lot more than cups of tea in bed to repay her.